The Encyclopaedia of
Pole Fishing

The Encyclopaedia of Pole Fishing

by Kevin Ashurst and Colin Graham

PELHAM BOOKS

First published in Great Britain by
Pelham Books Ltd
44 Bedford Square
London WC1B 3DP
1983
Reprinted 1984; 1985; 1986

Typeset by Cambrian Typesetters, Aldershot
Printed in Great Britain by
Hollen Street Press, Slough
and bound by
Dorstel Press Ltd, Harlow

British Library Cataloguing in Publication Data

Ashurst, Kevin
　　The encyclopaedia of pole fishing.
　　1. Fishing
　　I. Title　　II. Graham, Colin 1929
　　799.1'2　　　SH439

　　ISBN 0-7207-1449-4

Contents

Illustrations

Credits

All photographs are reproduced by permission of Angling News Services Ltd with the exception of the following: fig 12 Jordon Whiting; figs 51 & 61 Rodney S. Coldron; fig 55(6) Victor Borlandelli. The line drawings are by C.S. Jackson.

Preface

In another book written in co-operation with Kevin Ashurst (*World Class Match Fishing*), my colleague, Colin Dyson, wrote these opening words: 'If I had to elect somebody to fish for my life, I would undoubtedly choose Kevin Ashurst'. As one who has known Kevin even longer than Colin that statement seems as true for me today as it was for my colleague. Kevin remains simply the best all-round match angler this country has produced.

In attempting to produce a definitive volume about the value of pole fishing as a method for British anglers, there could surely be no better choice than Kevin Ashurst. While other English anglers have had pretensions to pole fishing greatness, they have usually tried to achieve this by slavishly imitating every nuance of the continental approach as exemplified by the French. But Kevin, so typically, watched and listened just as closely as his colleagues and instead of imitating what he saw, went on to incorporate new ideas of his own into the technique. Those ideas, of course, are present in this book and show clearly Kevin's ceaseless search for perfection in all things relevant to match angling.

As one who has seen nearly every World Championship for the past 20 years, my experience bridged what, for Kevin, was the vital period of the late 1960s and early 1970s. Indeed, I was there that shattering day in 1970 when Kevin fished his first World Championship. I have never seen him so utterly disconsolate. He will be telling you why later and of the effect this had on him.

In the meantime, I remain convinced that one of the

main reasons why pole fishing has come to be seen as the greatest alternative in the right circumstances to the rod and reel methods, favoured by British match anglers for so long, has been the unfailing enthusiasm of Kevin. This enthusiasm has been reflected from time to time in the angling press but is now gathered here in its entirety in one volume. It is our hope that you will agree that it *is* definitive.

As always, these things are not achieved without help — and this book is no exception. In no particular order, we would like to thank the following. First of all, our friends at the Northern Ireland Tourist Board in Belfast. When the book was commissioned, the English close season had just begun and it was clearly vital to have somewhere to fish, talk and take photographs in peace. For not by any means the first time, we ended up in Ulster's Lakeland in County Fermanagh, Kevin's idea, incidentally, of the nearest thing to paradise in the British Isles. As can be imagined, we were specially grateful for this invitation and particular thanks must go to Eric Thurley (for making all the arrangements in his usual efficient manner) and to Robbie Blair (the Board's fine photographer who took the excellent photograph which graces our cover). Next comes an old, old friend, Daniel Maury, editor of France's principal angling journal, 'La Pêche et les Poissons'. Daniel and I arranged the first ever friendly internationals between France and England and Kevin was one of my greatest supporters for the venture on this side of the English Channel. Daniel has given invaluable advice and inspiration. Last but by no means least, the man whose words opened this preface, Colin Dyson. As always in our little organisation, he has played devil's advocate with our text as an additional insurance against the possible omission of the kind of basic points which can so often be overlooked when two people have had to get as close to a subject as Kevin and I have with this one.

Colin Graham
Enniskillen, May 1982

Introduction

When I first started winning matches with some consistency in the 1950s and 1960s, I did so with the running line fished with rod and reel — the method long accepted by generations of English match anglers and rightly still used so often by them. If anybody had told me in those days that I would come to consider it equally vital to be able to fish with a pole, I would have thought them completely mad. Such an idea would never have crossed my mind and the same, I'm sure, went for every other angler. Poles, it was true, had been used long ago, especially by anglers fishing the Thames, but at the time in question they were regarded as extinct as the dodo.

At that time, of course, our continental friends were as devoted to pole fishing as we were to the rod and reel. That was something none of us knew or cared about, other than to hear once a year that there had been a World Championship match and that, as usual, it had been won by a continental team using poles. Looking back now, it seems strange and obviously raises the question, why didn't that success influence us then? I'm sure it's because even the finest English match anglers gave no thought to the World Championship, a total contrast to their attitude today! In my view, this was entirely due to the strange system then used by the National Federation of Anglers to pick our team for this event.

There was no selection committee or selector briefed to pick the best team on merit, as was the case in just about every other sport. Instead the six teams who finished at the top in the National Championships were entitled to nominate one man each to make up the squad for the following year's World Championship. If they wished, they could nominate one of the lesser talents in their team — and some did just that. Occasionally, of course, some of the great ones made it, the most notable example being the late Billy Lane, who became the first Englishman to become individual World Champion in 1963. But that, it would seem, was an exception and the chances of a team win seemed remote. In other words, membership of our World Championship team was simply an extra perk for those who did well in the National. Add the fact that, in those days, the National was settled solely on weight which often meant that a novice used the draw of a lifetime to win the Championship for himself (and sometimes for his team) and gain an automatic passport to the World Championship squad. With such a system, it was not likely we would ever field a team in which an attempt had been made to match the anglers to the water to be fished.

If you think that what I am saying is that no one in England took the World Championship seriously because of the system of selection, you are right though, I now cannot imagine why so little was said about it for so long. Certainly, I was as guilty as the rest. Though I could reasonably be said to have been a successful match angler throughout this period, I must admit I never gave it a thought . . . until 1970.

It happened like this. In 1969 I was a member of the Stoke City AA team captained by my father, which won the National Championship on the River Trent. Furthermore, I took the team's best weight from a peg on the Holme Marsh section of the river. The fact that Stoke had won meant that they were suddenly faced with nominating an angler to fish in the 1970 World Championship team. Like so many other teams at that time, they simply decided that the chance should go to the man who had taken the biggest weight in the National — me. I had no idea of what to expect. My name was sent off to the National Federation of Anglers and I was left to await developments.

The 1970 World Championship was fished on the Juliana Canal near Maastricht in Holland and the section chosen for the match was one of the most heavily fished pieces of water in the country. It was used weekly for fiercely contested matches involving anglers who, it transpired, fished entirely with the pole using bloodworm as bait. This part of the canal was within equally easy reach of anglers from Holland and Belgium and the rivalry between these two nations gave the contests added spice.

At that time, the NFA official in charge of the England team was the late Bernard Donovan, a popular figure in the Federation and a man who had been a member of the powerful Coventry AA team which had been so dominant in the National Championships in the 1950s. Bernard was keen to change the lackadaisical attitude England had towards the World Championships. At Bernard's insistence, Colin Graham managed to persuade one of our national newspapers to pay for a pre-match reconnaisance of the venue, the first time an England manager had ever had such an opportunity in the history of the match.

On that trip, Bernard naturally fished English methods for he knew he would be fielding a squad of men who would not have any confidence in fishing any other way. He caught fish and came back with several ideas for the match. Not long after this, I was told that we were to go there for the week before the event and practise on the sections of the canal which neighboured the match length, but not on the length itself. This was another new development for which Bernard must be credited. Previously, our teams had arrived immediately before the match, which meant they were virtually going into it blindfolded. Small wonder our results in the early days of the event were so poor!

During our welcome week's practice before this 1970 event, we fished intensively and I can remember being at first well content with our catches. While we had heard it was a bloodworm water, this was a bait none of us knew anything about though certain anglers in my home county of Lancashire regularly used it on the local canals. (This led to an outcry in certain quarters after the match about the fact that they should have been picked to fish it. This was the first indication that change was in the air with regard to the selection of the team.)

But we had no Lancashire bloodworm men with us and just had to do the best we could. It will be no surprise when I say that we first tried maggot, still the basic bait for most English match fishermen. We got nowhere and we concluded that this was because of the regularity with which the water had been fished with bloodworm. So we decided that perhaps caster, a bait becoming increasingly fashionable in England at that time, would be the thing to try. It was, after all, developed by anglers in the north-west and I, for one, was well aware that it was one of the only baits that would work in a water where bloodworm was universally fished.

We did well in practice with caster which, as you will discover, was a pity. I caught 12 lb (5.5 kg) in a timed trial over three hours, the duration of the World Championship. Even today, 12 lb would be an exceptionally good weight for any angler in most World Championships.

As the match approached, the die was becoming increasingly cast in favour of the caster, fished with the stick float, as our main method of attack. The combination of stick float and caster was, of course, *the* method at that time on the River Trent, our own premier match water.

But as the days went by, we began to have our doubts. We had taken those good weights on caster upstream of the match length but, when we moved to the downstream end of it, we discovered that we could catch next to nothing. The canal was difficult enough to fish anyway, because it was home to a string of big barges passing through every few minutes and because its movement varied constantly from stationary to a fast flow to flowing back.

So now, close to the moment of truth, we suddenly decided that although we had caught fish on the caster

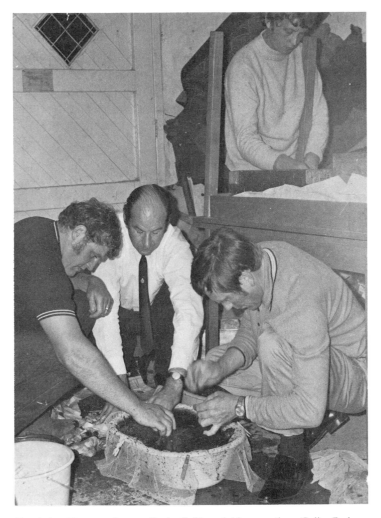

Fig. 1 In this rare picture, Kevin (left) and his co-author, Colin Graham (2nd left), work with other members of the England squad to clean the feeble supply of bloodworms flown out for the 1970 World Championships in Holland.

above the match length, we *must* have bloodworm and jokers, the latter being the small bloodworm which are used as feeders with their bigger brothers.

Norman Hayes, Coventry AA's nominee in the team, and I were deputed to try and find a stream in the area

15

which would produce jokers, a task which proved easier than we expected as the first friendly local we asked told us where they could be found. Bloodworms, however, are not so easy to find and it was eventually decided that we would have a supply of two pints (one litre, a truly minute quantity in the light of one's knowledge today!) flown out from England to Schiphol airport at Amsterdam.

Bernard drove across Holland to collect them and, as soon as he got back, we began the job of getting our strange bait into what we hoped would be a fit state for the match. We sieved the stuff in the cellar of our hotel well out of sight of the proprietor! Little did we know that all these frantic last-minute efforts still added up to the fact that we didn't have a hope.

In the match itself, we were absolutely annihilated and it's clear to me now that we still wouldn't have come within a mile of winning even if we had had gallons and gallons of bloodworms and jokers at our disposal.

Of the 12 teams fishing, England finished eighth, the remaining four being considered even bigger also-rans than us. The winners were Belgium, pole anglers to a man and led, as individual champion, by a man I still rate one of the most elegant pole anglers I've ever seen, Marcel van den Eynde. The home side, Holland, were second in a match in which that weekly rivalry on the water I mentioned earlier was vigorously renewed.

Our best individual in the field of 60 was Norman Hayes who was 24th with eight fish for 837 grammes. The lowest place achieved by any member of the England team on that fateful day — a miserable 47th — was me. I had five fish for 325 grammes. The only thing I can say in mitigation is that it was clear that I was drawn in the poorest section in the match. You can tell how bad it was when I add that Henri Guienheuf, the Frenchman who was individual champion in 1966, was second in the section at the next peg to me and that still put him only 19th in the individual list.

Fig. 2 Framed by the washing on a passing barge, Kevin fishes his first World Championship in Holland — the day he says he will never forget.

I can never remember being more devastated in my life and yet I remain eternally grateful for this experience. As I'm sure you will have guessed by now, the reason why I decided to recall this occasion in such detail was that this was the day this English angler first discovered that the pole was very much more than a toy with which some continental anglers played.

I went over and over the happenings in this match in my mind in the days which followed and I became totally convinced that the success of the continentals lay not in their bloodworm bait (though that was still important), but in the way their poles had permitted them to present it to the fish — positively, delicately and with total control. As you can imagine, I vowed I would never be caught out like this again.

But as any experienced match angler will tell you, old habits (especially those which impart confidence) die hard though, as I hope to demonstrate, this has not been altogether a bad thing. While we were foolish to remain so slavishly devoted to the rod and reel approach, it is now clear that the continentals were equally wrong to stick so single-mindedly to the pole.

When I got home from Holland in 1970, I was sick in my mind over what I felt had been the greatest failure in my life. I had so convinced myself I was capable of winning the match, I could not bring myself to believe that, far from winning, I had, in fact, produced the team's poorest result. I didn't want to eat, drink, be sociable or do anything, but dwell on my failure to grasp that there was a winning match fishing method that I had allowed myself to overlook. Thankfully, such depressions can lift and, in my case, the cloud lifted with the personal resolution that I was going to do nothing but fish with the pole until I knew what it was all about. No continental angler was going to beat me again!

I began my course of self-tuition on the canals which surround my home town of Leigh in Lancashire, concentrating in the bait department on caster, simply because it was the winning bait at the time. I saw no reason why it shouldn't win still more often if it was presented with a pole.

As any match angler will tell you, however, keenness is soon blunted in our kind of fishing if results are not produced reasonably quickly. While I remained convinced I had the right method, things changed on our canals, so much so that, suddenly, the pole did not seem the good idea it had been.

Bernard Donovan, incidentally, had given me the pole I was using, his last words being a request that I should look after it carefully. It was this pole I was using one winter day when I lost a section in the canal, having fitted it too carelessly together. I stripped to the buff and dived into the icy canal to recover it so fearful was I at the possibility of having to report the loss to Bernard. I recovered the missing piece, at the same time developing new respect for those who decide to go exploring in places like Antarctica!

But I digress. What happened on our canals was that, suddenly, they became as clear as gin everywhere and the fish became tightly shoaled for safety and always close to the bank opposite to where one was fishing. The pole Bernard had lent me was a maximum of 8 m in length (the longest available at that time) and I was no longer able to make contact with fish using this method. This was the first stage in what I now consider an unfortunate decline in my resolution to become master of the pole.

When it became equally obvious that I was not going to gain a place in the 1971 World Championship team (Stoke had finished out of the first six in the 1970 National Championship), I regret to admit that my enthusiasm was reduced still further.

In 1971, however, came a dramatic change. The NFA decided to end the haphazard system they had used for selecting their team. Bernard Donovan had died suddenly at the age of only 46 and his place was taken by Stan Smith, another angler who had, at one time, been a member of the famous Coventry team and who had also fished in some of the early World Championships. Stan managed to persuade the NFA that they should change their system to one of selection by invitation and British match fishing owes him a debt of gratitude for this act alone.

The new system came into force for the picking of the 1972 team. The match was to be fished on the River Berounka near Prague in Czechoslovakia. I was naturally honoured when I was invited to fish and, of course, I accepted.

Practice for this match was to be as it had been in Holland in 1970, during the week immediately before the event itself. Stan Smith, while not opposed to the pole method, remained convinced at this time that the rod and reel must be our approach, simply because he knew that none of us had the kind of pole fishing experience that would be likely to defeat the better continental sides.

Imagine our delight when we got to Czechoslovakia to find that the river was tailor-made for the rod and reel. Without doubt, this was to be England's greatest chance yet and it couldn't have come at a better time, the first occasion on which we had a hand picked team.

Sadly, we didn't win. France, the team who have won more times than any other, took the title but England finished second, our best ever result, and I was fortunate enough to win my section, in total contrast to my fate in 1970.

To our minds, the pole shouldn't have had a chance but, of course, the French used the pole. At the same time, it could be argued that we were handicapped in that no angler was then allowed to use more than 15 m of line in the World Championships (a ridiculous requirement and one which, happily, no longer exists thanks to the efforts of Stan Smith and the NFA). In this 1972 match, however, I don't think it really mattered. It could be said that if we had fished further out with our rods and reels with un-limited line, we could have beaten the French but, in all honesty, the line we fished was the one we wanted to fish and the French, with their longest poles, were able to fish it, too.

We were drawn next peg but one to them and the Frenchman near me was the man I still regard as their greatest pole angler, Guy Hébert. To say he matched me fish for fish for the first two and a half hours of this three hour event is not only an understatement, it's just not true. To my absolute amazement he was ahead of me for most of the time and it was only in the last ten minutes of the match, when I caught a few sizable roach and skimmers, that I managed to overtake him. There was only 8 oz (226 g) in it and I finished fourth individually with Guy fifth.

The most important thing was that a further lesson had been rammed home for anyone interested to learn from it – that the pole could win on a flowing river.

The 1973 match was on a lake near Chalons-sur-Soane in France. Still learning with the pole, we decided it was a

Fig. 3 Belgium's Marcel van den Eynde – the Belgian pole angler Kevin rates as one of the greatest – swings in a fish during the 1973 World Championships in France.

waggler water and we weren't far wrong. Belgium won with France second, both with the pole, and we were third . . . still close but, for us, not close enough.

It was, however, the following year's World Championship on the Watersportsbahn at Ghent in Belgium which, in my view, was the decisive one. We knew from the outset that it was not only a bloodworm water but also one which demanded that this bait be fished exclusively with the pole and nothing else. This meant that this was the first time that an England team would go into a World Championship

Fig. 4 Kevin in action in the 1974 World Championships at Ghent, Belgium

Fig. 5 Close-up of the actual tackle Jacie Morziéres gave to Kevin at the end of the 1974 World Championships; this tackle greatly influenced Kevin's pole thinking.

totally committed to fishing with the pole. I think it fair to add that that one decision did as much to emphasise the value of the pole to match anglers back home in England as anything else.

Again, we didn't get it right. We were sixth and the match was won once more by France. It still remained a memorable day for me. The Frenchman close to me in my section was Jackie Morziéres, an absolute wizard with the pole and one of France's greatest competitors. Jackie won the section three pegs away from me and, when the match was over, I went to congratulate him. His reply was to disconnect the tackle he had been using from his pole and present it to me as a gift. It was like being given at least one of the keys of the kingdom.

Though I had, of course, continued to fish the pole at home, that one small gesture by Jackie finally made up my mind for me. When I got back to England, I threw myself into the most intensive practice programme with the pole, a period which, I like to think, led me to the last and most important stage in my development as a pole angler.

My first success using an adaptation of Jackie's tackle (of which more later) was a second placing in a 300-peg winter open on the Trent at Holme Marsh with 14 lb (5 kg) of gudgeon, a catch that was widely reported in the angling press as the first real evidence that the pole might win matches in England.

Soon after this, I proved the point by winning a 400-peg open on the Lancaster Canal with pole and bloodworm . . . the first time that the method had won a match anywhere in this country.

I am flattered to be able to add that, as a result of that win, hundreds followed my example and there seems little doubt that this event gave the already developing accept-ance of the pole its biggest boost. It was certainly important for me because in the months leading up to that win, anglers had been laughing at me for persevering with what they called, 'the method that would never win'.

If I seem to have dwelt at some length on these events, this is because I like to hope that it will offer any angler all the evidence he needs to realise that the pole really is here to stay on this side of the English Channel, and that no match angler with any pretensions to consistency can afford to be unable to fish effectively with a pole.

Having, I hope, set the scene in a way which has con-vinced you to read on, let me now add that while the rest of this book is devoted entirely to the pole and how best to fish it, it should never be considered that the pole might become a substitute for the traditional English rod and reel methods — far from it.

What the events I described earlier taught me, and especially the World Championships, was, that it's very definitely not a case of one method being better than the other. The certain truth that emerged was that on certain days at certain places, the rod and reel will be the best method, while on other days at these places, the pole will be the best. It follows that the angler who can fish both methods well is twice as well equipped as the man who can perform well with only one.

Fig. 6 The kind of pole battery which is a common sight at any World Championship.

I can assure you, for instance, that this lesson was not lost on the French. After years of fishing solely with the pole, they became keen converts to our approach, so much so that in France today they now stage special matches where the rules demand that every competitor *must* fish with rod and reel or be disqualified, the best possible indication of their determination to become masters of the method as quickly as possible. As I said earlier, the French were just as wrong in sticking rigidly to the pole as we were in remaining solely loyal to the rod and reel. In my view, there has been no greater lesson learnt in match fishing in modern times.

For the newcomer to pole fishing, what, he will ask, are the considerations which decide him whether to fish as he has always done − or whether to use the pole?

The simplest answer I can give to this extremely important question − and I emphasise that it is a broad generalisation − is this. Accepting that the maximum range you can *comfortably* fish with the pole is 8 m, then any fishing to be done within that range must be more effective with the pole because the basic purpose of the pole is to *simplify* fishing. The only exception to this generalisation would be a swiftly flowing river.

Of course, these days the pole can be fished beyond 8 m but these longer ranges are for the pole specialist and newcomers would be well advised to confine their first efforts to the shorter ranges.

It follows that any fishing done beyond these ranges is best done with rod and reel. In other words, the pole does have its limits and the most important one is this question of range.

This will become more apparent in the chapters which follow. In the meantime, I hope I have given a basic perspective for an approach to this technique. I certainly guarantee that once you try the pole, you will come to enjoy it for its own sake, something few English anglers would have dreamed of saying as recently as 1978, the year when, in my view, the pole penny really began to drop on a large scale for anglers here in England.

1 The Pole Method and How It Works

Ask me to give a basic description of the pole method and the most apt reply, I think, would be to liken it to most people's remembrance of a child's fishing tackle – a cane, a cork, a piece of string and a bent pin. Though the pole methods we are going to discuss are now winning matches all over the country and are much more sophisticated than anything a child would use, it doesn't alter the fact that the principle is the same: you are fishing with line fixed to a stiff rod with a hook and a float.

Using a pole, the reel is dispensed with. The pole itself should be as rigid as possible and, for the greatest versatility, as long as possible, though beginners would be wise not to attempt to fish at the longest ranges in their 'L-plate' period.

In the simplest form of pole fishing, the line is tied direct to the tip of the pole, usually to a loop of nylon line whipped onto the tip (see Fig. 7). Below is the float, the weights needed to cock it, and the hook. This usage of the pole is known as the flick tip method and I favour it whenever possible.

When fishing with the continental style floats now generally available on the British tackle market, it's considered best to fish with the tip of the pole directly above the float with the distance between the two not more than 2 ft (60 cm); this is known as short lining.

If you think about it, this will mean that the tip of the pole is as directly above the bait on the hook as possible.

Fig. 7 Nylon loop fitted to top of flick tip pole.

This also means that you strike simply by lifting the pole, so that this movement is much more positive than it would be with a rod and reel, where the first thing the strike must achieve *before* reaching the fish is to remove the angle of line between rod, float and hook.

It's this difference which has led to general agreement that the flick tip system of pole fishing offers the most positive strike you are ever likely to get in any style of fishing, from which it follows that you have a much better chance of hooking fish, thus reducing the ratio of missed bites.

There are variations on this basic approach and these will be examined in detail later when we discuss all the methods that can be used but there is one which should be mentioned in this basic part of our text. Where big fish are likely to be encountered (and I am thinking of fish up to 3 lb (1.3 kg) in weight) then a change must be made in the set-up just described.

This is the introduction of a 9–18 in (22–45 cm) length of elastic between the tip of the pole and the top of the line. I hope it will not need me to tell you that the purpose of the elastic is to act as a shock absorber when a big fish is hooked, such a fish being likely to snap a line tied directly to the pole (the flick tip method) because clearly there is less give in this tackle.

The other advantage of the elastic is that it automatically ensures that a tight line is maintained between the pole and the fish at all times. If the fish moves away, the elastic stretches. If the fish turns back, it contracts. The use of elastic is known in France as the *methode Roubaisienne* because this simple but brilliant idea was invented by some anglers who lived in Roubaix.

Elastics (Fig. 8) are available in a variety of strengths, the strength to be used depending on the breaking strain of the hook length to be linked to the pole by the main line and the elastic. Obviously, the pole angler needs a selection of these in various strengths and in the table I recommend examples described as strong, medium and fine.

There is a strength described as extra fine which some people consider useful. I am not one of them because I find this elastic has so much stretch that it can often become impossible to exercise any kind of control over a fish. Furthermore, even when a comparatively small fish is refusing to be coaxed in and has streteched the elastic

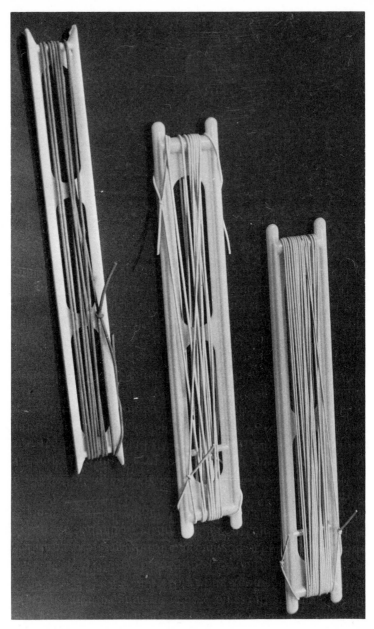

Fig. 8 Elastic in the three strengths recommended by Kevin: strong, medium and fine.

to its maximum, the line will suddenly yield and, instead of being smoothly retrieved, the fish will spring out of the water so that it can be lost.

Recommended line and elastic strengths for match fishing with the pole

	Still waters	*Canals*	*Rivers*
Easy waters			
Main line	2.5 lb (1.1 kg)	2.0 lb (907 g)	3.0 lb (1.3 kg)
Hook length	1.5 lb (680 g)	1.5 lb (680 g)	2.0 lb (907 g)
Elastic (if needed)	strong	strong	strong
Hard waters			
Main line	1.5 lb (680 g)	2.0 lb (907 g)	2.0 lb (207 g)
*Hook length	1.0 lb (450 g)	**1.0 lb (450 g)	1.0 lb (450 g)
Elastic (if needed)	medium	medium	medium
Difficult waters			
Main line	1.0 lb (450 g)	1.0 lb (450 g)	2.0 lb (907 g)
Hook length	8–12 oz (226–340 g)	8–12 oz (226–340 g)	1.0 lb (450 g)
Elastic (if needed)	fine	fine	medium

* Though it shouldn't need saying, the hook length must *always* be a lighter breaking strain than the main line when fishing with the pole. If you get snagged or broken by a fish, this guards against the loss of the entire tackle and the time it takes to replace it. With lines matched as recommended, only the hook length should need replacement in such circumstances.
** If big fish are likely to be encountered in this setting, this hook length should be stepped up to 1.5 lb (680 g).

Pause now and consider the vital ingredients for this method: the elastic, its length, and the strength dictated by the calibre of *hook length* being used. How do you marry all these together?

The yardstick for the relationship between these two

factors is this: 8–12 oz (226–340 g) breaking strain hook length (fine elastic), 1 lb–1½ lb (450–680 g) (medium), 2 lb plus (907 g) (strong).

I realise there are some who insist on using the extra fine elastic (usually with a 4 oz (113 g) hook length). I repeat; I consider it irrelevant simply because a man reduced to such limits can have little chance of winning a match in this country, while an angler using a pole simply for pleasure would surely never want to fish like this.

The other decision to be made involves the length of the elastic which, you will recall, should be between 9 and 18 in (22–45 cm). The yardstick here is, the lighter the line being used the longer the elastic should be up to the maximum of 18 in (45 cm). An elastic of the latter length is capable of extension to 6 ft (1.8 m).

The French used to increase the strength of the elastic by putting a number of twists into it (Fig. 9) but this practice is becoming less common because the wider variety of elastic strengths now available renders it unnecessary.

Fig. 9 Twisted elastic like this is designed to increase strength, but Kevin thinks it is no longer necessary.

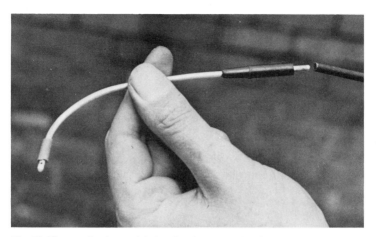

Fig. 10 The metal pole crook being fitted to the pole. If yours is made of fibreglass this is equally efficient.

When an elastic shock absorber is being employed with a pole, the generally accepted method of fitting it is to connect it to a metal or fibreglass crook fixed to the tip of the pole (Fig. 10). A loop is tied in the top end of the elastic and this loop is then placed in the slot in the crook, being finally secured by locking it into position with a collar of plastic (Fig. 11). Whether your pole has a metal or fibreglass crook will depend on the make you select; there's no difference in efficiency, so you can use either type with confidence.

Latterly, some hollow crooks have become available (Fig. 12) with the elastic housed inside the tube of the

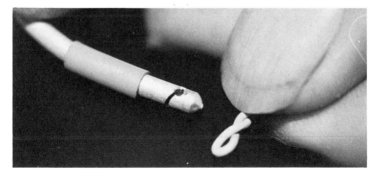

Fig. 11 Fixing elastic to the crook: a) note plastic sleeve.

33

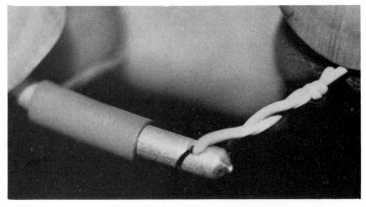

b) the elastic is placed in the slit.

c) the elastic is secured by moving the plastic sleeve down over the slit.

crook. They are neatly made and their advantage is that they guard against the elastic tangling round the end of the pole, something which, as you will discover, can happen very easily indeed when fishing with this method.

Neat as they are, I don't favour these crooks, mainly because the length of elastic that can be housed in them is not long enough to provide the same degree of protection against a break as can be obtained with the elastics you make up yourself for use with the open crook; but I do think the buckle swivel link for fixing the main line to the elastic in our picture (see Fig. 12 again) is an excellent idea. With this fitting entire tackles can be changed much

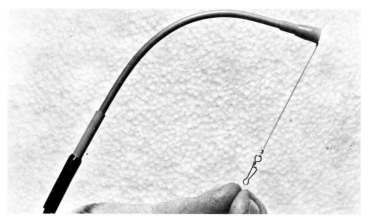

Fig. 12 Pole crook with elastic fixed inside. Note the buckle swivel for attaching the main line, an advantage for any pole tackle.

quicker because the need to link the two with a knot is eliminated.

As I said earlier, I prefer to fish the flick tip method (ie with no elastic) whenever possible because of the positive strike it offers. With the elastic, the strike is less positive because of the slightly delayed action the elastic gives to this important movement.

Nevertheless, I do use elastics. I have to for, like every other angler, I may encounter fish too strong to be netted with the flick tip method. I have reservations about the usefulness of elastic and, based on a great deal of experience, I feel it is very important to consider them.

The first concerns fishing with the metal crook. This is efficient but only if you are fishing not more than 5 m from the bank. Beyond that range, the slightest judder or jerk communicated to the pole causes an instant tangle of the elastic round the crook. But there is one exception. A crook will still remain tangle free *beyond* 5 m if heavy tackle is being used, ie a float carrying not less than the equivalent in weight of three AAA shots. This amount of lead is enough to keep the elastic away from the crook when casting.

So what if we want to fish beyond 5 m but we are *not* using reasonably heavy float tackle? What then? My answer, and it's one of the best dodges I have discovered, is something I learnt from the Belgians. They, like me, prefer the flick tip method whenever they can get away with it but they, too, find that sometimes elastic is a must. Their answer is to use a much longer elastic than usual. They pass this down through a hole in the tip of the pole, locking the end in position down the pole with a peg at the base of the first or second section from the top. This means that the length of elastic being employed is now anything from 2–6 ft (60 cm – 1.8 m) long.

Before describing the very real advantage of this, let me describe the way this is incorporated into the pole. First of all (Fig. 13), it is necessary to doctor the end of the pole by creating an aperture smooth enough to ensure that, when drawn from the pole by a fish, the elastic will be subject to the least possible friction. I achieve this by mounting a piece of strong plastic tubing on the pole tip with the walls of the mouth rounded off at the aperture. The upper end of the elastic is prevented from slipping back down the pole by the use of a stopper (see Fig. 13 again), the elastic being linked to the main line by a buckle swivel (see Fig. 12 again). The other end of the elastic is held in place at the lower end of the first or second section of the pole by a plastic plug (Fig. 14).

What are the advantages of this system? First, it completely eliminates the problems of elastic tangling round

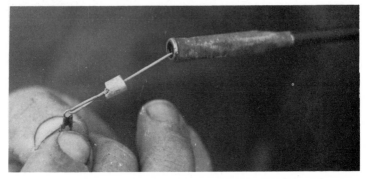

Fig. 13 End of pole with elastic fitted in top section. Notice the stopper and buckle swivel (held in the fingers) to allow easy tackle changing.

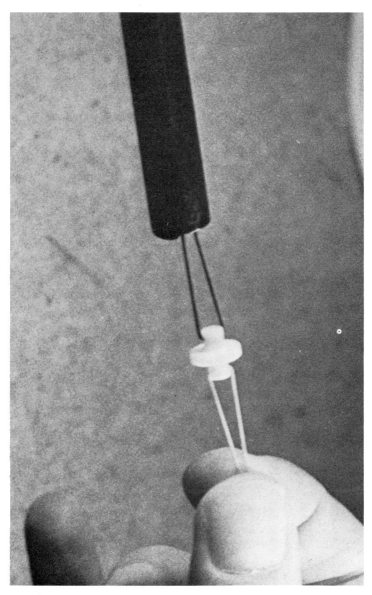

Fig. 14 The plug used at the lower end of the pole sections through which an elastic has been fixed. Again notice the stopper. Since the text of this book was completed, some tackle makers now offer pole tops complete with elastics fitted in this way.

the crook for we have now disposed entirely of the latter. Secondly, and much more important, it gives us much greater leeway with those bigger fish. The 2–6 ft (60 cm– 1.8 m) elastic can stretch to a tremendous length compared with those we discussed earlier for use with the crook. These longer elastics can extend to 12 ft (3.6 m) thus vastly increasing the shock absorbing capabilities of the entire tackle. It will still be difficult to subdue a fish of more than 3½ lb (1.5 kg), but remember we are now fishing at range (ie beyond the 5 m maximum I specified for the crook) and if, for instance, a 10 m pole was being used you could play a sizable fish over the entire length of the normal match peg, and still be certain of netting it.

In this chapter, I have sought to restrict myself to a definition of basic principles for it is important these are clearly understood at the outset. There are, of course, many more matters of detail involved and, as we discuss them in later chapters, you'll discover how best to employ these basic points, especially when they are linked to the accessories that are needed and, more important still, the way each tackle is made up to provide the widest possible application of the pole system.

2 The Poles Themselves

Anyone who doubts that the pole revolution is here to stay should simply walk into the nearest fishing tackle shop and, if it is any good, he will see dozens of them for sale. As recently as the mid 1970s you would have been unlikely to see a single one in most areas.

Unfortunately, as so often happens when a new trend emerges in fishing tackle, manufacturers seek to flood the market in a bid to get the biggest share of the new business and, equally this means there's a great variation in quality. This is just as true for poles as it is for any other commercial goods.

As a really good pole of 12 m in carbon fibre, the 'in' material for all fishing rods these days, can cost more than £500, the question of quality is of the greatest importance and, for the novice, that of price equally so.

As I write, incidentally, there's already much talk about the potential of a new material for poles called boron. The odd, very expensive fly rod is already on the market in this substance but my information is that it has not been the success that was hoped for and I would urge you to treat any development of this for poles with the utmost caution. The main problem, I've heard, is that while extra lightness has been achieved with boron, an advantage with any pole, there has been difficulty allying this quality with strength and durability.

To an angler who has decided to take up pole fishing for the first time, I would say that it is not necessary to spend a lot of money on his first pole. Furthermore, it needn't be in carbon fibre.

I would suggest a pole of 8 m in fibreglass as a good first purchase. Such a weapon of good quality can be obtained for as little as £30, not too big an outlay, I reckon, for something of such importance to an angler, especially a match angler. Indeed, there are now so many poles in circulation, it could well be that you could thus further reduce your initial cost by buying a spare from a friend.

Having bought an 8 m pole, do *not* attempt to fish at its full range from the start. That could put you off for life for it's definitely something you've got to get used to handling, so cumbersome can it seem at first. My advice would be to begin by fishing at a maximum range of 5m. Once you feel you are fishing confidently and easily at that distance, increase your range a metre at a time until, eventually, you will come to be able to fish the full 8 m without strain. Once you have reached that target, you're bound to have become a pole convert, otherwise you wouldn't have persevered until this stage was reached.

The next thing you will want to do now is to fish with an even longer pole and it's at this stage that you will begin to consider whether you should invest in carbon fibre, especially if, by now, you are pole fishing regularly. If you are a match angler and consider yourself good enough to be picking up money fairly regularly then there should be no hesitation about this decision.

The advantage of carbon fibre, of course, is its lightness compared to fibreglass. Though fibreglass poles are available in lengths greater than 8 m, they are very heavy indeed. Not only are they unwieldy, however, their action is no longer satisfactory. By contrast, the carbon fibre pole gives you so much lightness, you can fish with the same comfort at 10 m in this material as you could at 8 in fibreglass, probably more so. It is, of course, a big investment and I can only say that if you are ever to become a complete pole angler you will have to take this step eventually. In terms of pain in the pocket, I am reminded of a good match angler in Lancashire whose pay did not permit him to buy a carbon pole. He took the unusual step of approaching his bank manager for a loan, offering his skill as collateral. He got the loan and had paid the bank back within three months! Perhaps your listening bank manager will lend a sympathetic ear to a similar tale if you consider it necessary.

Let's pause a moment now to consider certain characteristics of the poles themselves. At one time, and it wasn't so very long ago either, it was regularly said that to be any good a pole had to be as rigid as a poker throughout its length, exactly the reverse of the quality one would look for in a rod for use with a reel. However, poles were not nearly as well made then as they are now and that was the main reason for the validity of that statement. These days, it's no longer so true and, in certain circumstances, this may be ignored. A pole that was whippy was always considered a bad buy. It still can be, but if the pole in question is not more than 5m long then a certain amount of whippiness should not cause any problems. Beyond 5 m, and certainly at lengths like 10 m in carbon fibre, it is absolutely essential that the pole be reasonably stiff and certainly not whippy in any way. The reason for this is that whippiness beyond 5 m starts to interfere with the pole's most important characteristic, its positive strike. This is doubly true in those situations when you are fishing with the float close to the pole, the short line position.

Another important factor is a pole's diameter. Again in the not too distant past, the longest poles had enormous butts, so much so that the description 'bargepole' so often given them was totally accurate. They were far from easy to handle. Today, the manufacturers seem to have gone a long way to meet the justified demand for smaller diameters without any loss of power. So this is another point you should bear in mind when choosing your pole. Make sure the butt is not too thick for you to handle comfortably. And don't forget that the smaller the diameter of your pole, the less resistance it will offer when it's windy, this being of the greatest advantage when fishing at the longest ranges. Check, too, that the joints fit easily. They should be not too loose and not too firm.

Finally, always favour what is called the take-apart pole, the type that can be broken down into its sections simply by removing each section from the bottom. This cannot be done with the other type, the telescopic pole, which is why, basically, I have no use for the latter. The only conditions in which I can see them having any value is for fishing at extremely close range for small fish like bleak.

Having bought your pole, the next job is to learn how to handle it and this is easy enough provided you bear in mind the simple basic movements required and the first is the cast.

There are four basic casts with the pole. The first (Fig. 15) is casting from the groin. The butt of the pole is supported here and the hand controlling the pole is used to swing the tackle gently out to the baited area. Next, the underhand cast (Fig. 16). The pole is held with one hand and with the pole at an angle of about 45°, the tackle is again swung out to the chosen spot. A variation on this theme (Fig. 17) is the underhand cast with two hands, this being more likely the longer the pole that is being used. Again, the movement is a smooth underhand swing with the aim of ensuring that the tackle lands lightly on the water. Fourth and last is the overhead cast (Fig. 18), which is needed when the cast is being made against a wind or stiffish breeze. With this cast, the tackle is swung behind and the pole stopped in the vertical position before the tackle is projected forward. I have not gone into great detail about these casts for I think our pictures tell you most of what you need to know. The most important cautionary note to strike is to warn you against 'snatching' on the cast – especially when an elastic attached to a crook is being used – as this can result in tangles round the end of the pole. They're usually easy enough to disengage . . . but they're time wasting. Tell yourself from the time you first begin handling your pole that what you are attempting is easier than it would be with rod and reel and you'll soon relax and achieve that smoothness of movement I mentioned earlier which is so essential for pole efficiency.

42

Fig. 15 Casting with the butt of the pole supported in the groin.

After the cast, there are two ways in which the pole should be held while waiting for the bite you hope will follow. Which of these stances you adopt is decided by whether you are fishing at such short range it's unnecessary to take the pole apart to get the fish in (what pole anglers

43

Fig. 16 Making the underhand cast with one hand.

call unshipping the pole), or whether you are fishing with line of such an exact length that after you have hooked the fish the line length will enable you to swing it directly to your free hand.

Let's consider the first of these alternatives – the capture of fish which demand that the pole be unshipped. The ideal

Fig. 17 The underhand cast – using both hands.

Fig. 18 The overhead cast. The pole is brought back to the vertical position before being projected forward for the final stage of the cast.

stance (Fig. 19) is to sit comfortably with the pole resting across the thigh and held in both hands as shown, this stance is more likely the greater the range that is being fished. If, alternatively, you are lifting fish straight from the water to your hand with a long pole, then the butt of the pole should be supported in the groin (Fig. 20) and held with one hand only.

Your next movement is dictated by the strike which follows the bite. When you watch an angler strike at range when fishing with rod and reel, the movement is often really violent with the rod travelling through a considerable arc. Because of the pole's striking efficiency, there's nothing like the need for violent movement. Whichever of the waiting stances you've adopted (Figs. 19 and 20), it's simply necessary to lift the hook into the fish and not to ram it in. In terms of movement, the only thing to consider is its direction. If you are fishing at range (and especially if you are fishing at range with the short line), the pole should always be held in front of you and the strike should

Fig. 19 Pole stance for fishing at range.

47

Fig. 20 The pole supported in the groin. The same method of support can also be used in a seated position.

always be vertical, ie you are literally lifting the baited hook into the fish's mouth (Fig. 21). This is the normal strike and the one the pole angler uses for 90 per cent of the time. The exception is when you are fishing a waggler, ie a float attached at the bottom only. With this type of float, it's best to strike by moving the pole, again gently, to the right or left, the direction being simply the one that suits you best (Fig. 22). This strike is particularly efficient if, in addition to the use of the waggler, the fish are taking the bait as it falls through the water (ie on the drop). The sideways strike in this instance prevents the fish being brought to the surface too quickly and thereby causing the kind of disturbance which might persuade the rest of the shoal they would be wiser to look elsewhere for something to eat.

Next is the most important bit of business of all – getting the fish safely to the net. Consider first a situation where

Fig. 21 The vertical strike.

Fig. 22 Striking sideways.

you are fishing at range with a short line (say a range of 10 m with 3 m of line being employed between pole tip and hook). Immediately the fish is hooked, the pole should be moved slightly to one side (left or right) and then threaded back through the hands onto the bank until the point is reached at which the pole can be separated at that section which means that when the remaining upper sections are lifted the fish can be swung directly to the hand. I've seen some anglers carrying out this unshipping movement section by section until the desired one is reached. There's nothing wrong in that if bankside obstructions demand it but it's much quicker to get used to judging precisely where to make the break to get the fish straight to hand because so much time is saved (Fig. 23). Equally important when unshipping a pole, again especially at range, is to

Fig. 23 a) A fish is hooked and the pole is fed back through the hands:

b) the pole is broken at the point which permits the fish to be brought to hand;

c) the unshipped sections are laid down to permit the fish to be swung in.

ensure that as you feed the lower sections behind you they rest firmly on the ground and are not leaning in such a way that the pole is capable of bending severely under its own weight. In these circumstances it's always possible the pole could snap, a very expensive occurrence for the carbon

Fig. 24 When a long length of pole is laid down, it should be rested on the ground as shown, to prevent breakage.

fibre owner (Fig. 24). In all these movements, the aim should always be to ensure that the final one brings the fish to the hand (Fig. 25). If the line is just a little shorter than the pole, this can be done immediately after the strike. If not, unshipping is necessary.

The other situation which may occur, while bringing fish straight to hand or unshipping to achieve this, is that you can encounter an unexpectedly big fish. When this

Fig. 25 Provided the pole has been correctly shipped the fish will swing direct to the angler's hand.

happens, the best protection is to *add* any sections of the pole not in use because the range didn't demand it. It follows, I hope, that, because of this eventuality, you will have any remaining sections already assembled close to hand and will not have left yourself exposed to the need to begin putting them together while you have got the fish on. The extra length will give you an extra bit of control against any powerful fish but, of course, it is no guarantee. Equally, it follows that if the pole is fully assembled when this happens you've simply got to hold on . . . and hope.

These, then, are the basic movements for the pole angler. Once you have mastered them, you should have no problems, always provided that you accept that 3½ lb (1.5 kg) is the maximum weight of fish likely to be landed on a pole tackle.

3 Pole Accessories

Obviously, there's much more to pole fishing than just the pole itself. As always in angling, all sorts of ancillary items are needed and in this chapter I propose to describe them so that, by the time we begin to fit them together in various forms, you will be equipped in every way to try out the suggestions which are made later.

In the main, the pole is always fished with a float. It can be used for legering, but only with the float – something that you will discover is a fairly exceptional circumstance.

So the first thing you need is a selection of the right kind of floats for pole fishing. As the late Billy Lane said in his book, *The Encyclopaedia of Float Fishing* (Pelham Books), far too many of the floats on view in tackle shops are there to catch anglers and not fish. The same is regrettably true of the thousands of pole floats now finding their way into these same establishments.

It's important, therefore, to understand from the outset exactly which type of floats are worth adding to your tackle box and which should be eliminated, quite apart from any question of cost. For this reason, I am now going to describe all the floats I use, leaving any discussion of how and why I use them until later. In doing this, I think this is also a good moment to re-emphasise something I said in our opening chapter, because it remains one of the most important statements anywhere in this book. You will recall that I suggested that the continental anglers were just as mistaken in sticking solely to the pole for so long as we were in our total loyalty to the rod and reel.

It is now clear that it is necessary for anglers, especially match anglers, to be masters of both techniques. The French, easily the most consistent team in the World Championships and surely some of the finest pole anglers in the world, have got the message. They are busy, not just at international team level, but all over the country, developing their rod and reel techniques. As I said earlier, they're now even staging matches where every competitor must fish with a pole. It's not a bad way of persuading anglers that the old habits are far from necessarily the best.

But there's more to this and it's something every English writer I have read so far on this subject has ignored — and this is the second most important statement in this book. While more and more English anglers are rightly adopting the pole they are also adopting the methods in a way which is creating what must be considered an English (as opposed to the continental) dimension to the technique. Initially, we tried to marry our main float fishing methods, like the stick and the waggler, to their poles instead of starting with continental ideas. It was wrong but, understandable; and it has since developed to our credit. What we have now are English pole methods as well as continental ones and this has added to the technique's efficiency. The writers I have mentioned have striven to persuade English match anglers that they should base their approach only on an exact copy of the continental system. In doing so, they have done the sport a disservice and, in my view, at one time hampered the English developments. Happily, this has changed and I think we can expect still more from the ever increasing swing to the pole by more and more anglers on this side of the English Channel.

With that little digression off my chest, let's get back to the mainstream of our current discussion — the kind of floats needed to get the best results from your pole fishing. In my view, seven different patterns are essential for successful pole fishing and, in saying that, remember that not only do you need all these patterns, you need each of them in various sizes to enable you to fish them in different ways.

First, and what may be considered *the* basic pole float, is the pattern I call the balsa bristle (Fig. 26). This, to the best of my knowledge, was a French creation and was the pattern most used by that great match angler, Robert Tesse, the only man to become World Champion three times. The body is made of slimly shaped balsa and the tip is a nylon bristle. The float is fixed to the line top and bottom (what English anglers call 'double rubber', though rubbers aren't employed in this case). At the top, the float is engaged by passing the line through an eyelet ring fixed to the side near the top of the body (see Fig. 20 again). The main advantage of this (especially when the lighter patterns are being used) is that it encourages the float to sit as vertically as possible in the water. If you use a normal float rubber in this position, the float has a tendency to lean and even the small amount of air trapped by the rubber would delay the cocking of the float and might even require a coaxing lift from the pole to get it right. At the base of

Fig. 26 The balsa bristle.

the float, there is usually a short wire stem and the line is attached to this by means of a small plastic collar.

The second float pattern I consider necessary is the bodied bristle (Fig. 27). Though not likely to be used as much as most of the others, this is the logical place to mention it because of its relation to the balsa bristle. The float fulfils exactly the same functions as the balsa bristle and is fixed to the line in an identical manner, the difference being that the body allows you to fish with more weight down the line.

My third pattern, made of peacock quill with a wire stem, is what I call the gudgeon float though, as you will discover, it catches other species, too. My first experience of this float (Fig. 28) was at the 1974 World Championships in Belgium. Indeed, this was the very float that Jackie Morziéres presented to me at the end of this match after using it to win his section. It's a wonderful float in the right setting and I cannot commend it too highly. Like the balsa bristle, it's fastened to the line top and bottom by

Fig. 27 Bodied bristle.

Fig. 28 The gudgeon bristle.

the same method, a side ring at the top and the wire stem at the foot. As you will discover, it has its uses in many settings but especially on canals. The main advantage it offers is that whenever there is a surface flow or drag caused by the wind, this float is more stable than the balsa bristle which tends to ride too high for accurate bite indication.

Next is a float of my own design which, one might say, is one of the English developments. As it is not available in tackle shops, you will have to make some for yourself. I consider it a vital float and I call it simply the cocktail stick — because it's made with a cocktail stick and a piece of peacock quill (Fig. 29). Its construction is extremely easy. You put a dab of balsa cement on the tip of the cocktail stick and push this into the base of the peacock quill for ¼ in (6.3 mm) and the float is made, apart from painting it. While the cocktail stick is always the same length, I have a selection of floats with various lengths and diameters of peacock quill mounted on the stick. The length of quill varies from 1—2 in (2.5—5 cm) and in diameter

Fig. 29 The cocktail stick.

from ⅟₁₆ –⅛ in (1.5–3 mm). It's a stillwater float which I find invaluable for use in certain conditions. On a lake, you often find that a cross wind is blowing which has created an undertow in the water which is going in the opposite direction. In this situation, the floats I discussed earlier will move away from the spot where you have placed the feed to attract the fish in the direction of the wind. This float not only stays firmly put, it will go in the direction of the undertow if this is stronger than the wind and, while a moving float is not usually considered a good thing in still water, I can assure you that, in this situation, it is a winner. One more important thing about this float is that it can be fished with a long line (ie a longer distance between pole tip and float). This means it can be effectively fished *beyond* the pole tip instead of the more usual position directly underneath it.

Next is another float which, in the pole armoury, is also an English development. The float (Fig. 30) is one of the rod and reel angler's favourites, the straight peacock, in miniature. I call it the dibber. It's another you will have to make for yourself but, again, it's easy. The peacock body varies from 1–3 in (2.5–7.6 cm) in length, and in diameter from ⅛ in (3 mm) to the thickest quill you can get. Into the base of the quill, you push a ½ in (1.2 cm) long piece of ¹⁄₁₆ in (1.5 mm) diameter cane, again using a little balsa cement to seal the joint. The cane should be pushed carefully ¼ in (6.3 mm) into the peacock leaving the remaining half projecting. It is at the base of this cane projection that the float is held on the line with a normal float rubber. Two situations you will discover, lead me to use it. The first is when I want to fish heavier than the biggest the cocktail stick pattern will allow, and the other is when I want to lay the bait well over depth on the bottom.

Next a float (Fig. 31) that was designed in Germany and was used so successfully by the West Germans themselves in the 1980 World Championships on the River Neckar when they scored a devastating win. In the team match,

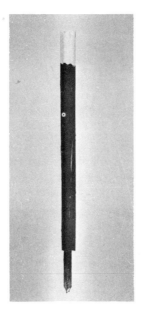

Fig. 30 The dibber.

Fig. 31 The bung float.

when points scored over the sections are absolutely vital as in our own National Championships, they had four winners from the five sections. The only section they didn't win was taken by yours truly . . . using this same float. I am sure I need say no more about its pedigree. I call this the bung float because it has a resemblance to the bung once so widely used by pike anglers. The bung is only for use with the pole in deep, flowing rivers, especially those where bream are likely to be caught. Like the balsa bristle and the gudgeon floats, it's fitted to the line at the top by passing the line through an eyelet ring fixed to the body. The accurate placing of this ring is most important. I mention this to warn you that there are examples on sale here where the ring is in the wrong position, so that the float simply won't fish correctly. The top ring on this float should be one third from the top of the body. If it is higher than that, it will give you trouble if you try to fish it. The float is fixed at the bottom with a plastic collar pushed onto the base of the wire stem.

The seventh and last float in my collection is one I use only when it is necessary to fish for bleak on the surface with the pole (Fig. 32). It is simply a 2 in (5 cm) long piece of plastic with a diameter of $^3/_{16}$ in (4.5 mm). At one time, anglers used to favour a similar shape in peacock quill for this purpose but I have found that plastic is much better, for two reasons. First, it gives casting weight on a line carrying no shots without putting the fish off and, secondly, and more importantly, it lifts easily from the surface. The floats I use were obtained from a tackle shop but whether they are still available I cannot say. They're easy enough to make if you can't find them and, obviously, they are only for occasional use.

If I have dwelt at some length on these floats compared with some other accessories, that is simply because the float is *the* most important thing you are going to use with your pole. Just before we go on to consider the other accessories which are necessary, may I remind you to make sure you get tip colours that suit your eyes. My own choice

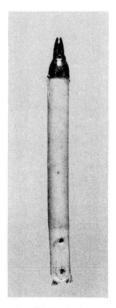

Fig. 32 Bleak float.

is for yellow or orange for dark backgrounds and black for light water backgrounds. And now those other necessary items.

First of all, you need a wide selection of plastic winders (Fig. 33) on which to store complete tackles made up ready for instant use, this being yet another example of how the pole simplifies fishing. The entire tackle (line, float, weights, and hook) is wrapped onto the winder after all the component parts have been properly matched quietly at home and, when unwound, can be fitted in seconds to the pole ready for use. It is useful to buy winders in different colours for you can use the colour as part of your personal code for telling exactly what tackle is on each winder. This is necessary to enable you to select the right one at a glance. Everybody has his own system for this but, for what it's worth, I'm sure there are three things which you need to know when picking a winder from your box, the length of the tackle (in metres), the strength of the line and the size of hook at the business end. Some anglers use small self-adhesive labels and simply put their marks on those with indelible ink, ie 7/2.5/1.5/20 tells you that the tackle on that winder is 7 m long. The main line is 2.5 lb (1.1 kg) breaking strain, the hook length 1.5 lb (680 g) and the hook, a 20. The winder colour can be used as a guide, too. The most common use relates to hooks; ie all red winders have 20 hooks on, all blue ones, 22s, and so on. How you do it is up to you, but it is important and it also shows the variety that exists for each pattern of float. The top French anglers, for instance, will have 100 different winders in their boxes with different combinations on them, and hundreds more at home for different waters. Personally, I don't think such numbers are necessary but, once you do get into pole fishing, you will find that you will want to carry an ever increasing number of tackles. After a while you will become familiar with exactly which patterns need carrying to the waters you fish regularly, almost without looking. One final point about winders. Always make sure that the winder is big enough to ensure that the float on

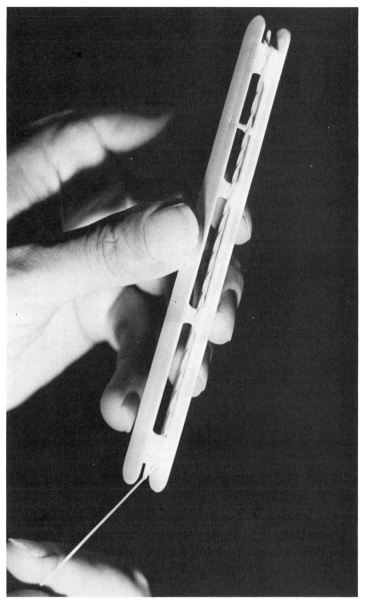

Fig. 33 The very useful winders on which pole tackles are stored.

that particular tackle does not protrude at either end of the winder. That way you could damage it and so render the entire tackle useless.

Next comes another most important item of tackle which stems from the continent, the Olivette lead (Fig. 34). These, without question, are one of the most useful things I have ever come across and they will be used at least 50 per cent of the time when pole fishing. At first, English anglers were resistant to them because they had always been taught to fish as lightly as possible near the hook. To them, it seemed an unacceptable contradiction that so

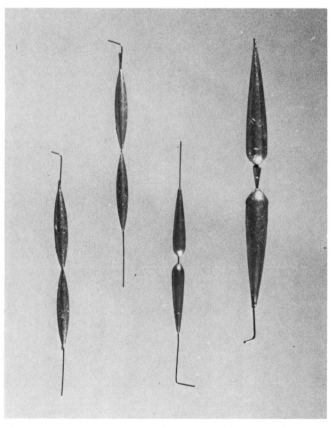

Fig. 34 Olivette leads: the pear-shaped leads on the right are Paquitas (the type mostly used by Kevin), those on the left, Comte-stix.

Comparison table of English lead shot and Olivettes by size and weight in grammes

Shot size	Weight	Olivette size (Paquita)	Weight	Olivette size (Torpille)	Weight
		12	3.0		
		11	2.45	11	2.5
		10	2.10	10	2.0
Swan	1.89				
		9	1.85	9	1.5
		8	1.56	8	1.2
		7	1.36	7	1.00
		6	1.16		
		5	0.82		
AAA	0.81				
				6	0.80
		4	0.67		
				5	0.60
				4	0.50
		3	0.44		
BB	0.40			3	0.40
		2	0.37	2	0.30
No 1	0.28				
		1	0.25		
No 3	0.20				0.20
No 4	0.17	0	0.17		
No 5	0.13	2/0	0.13	0	0.13
No 6	0.105	3/0	0.105		
No 7	0.083				
		4/0	0.081		
No 8	0.063				
*No 9	0.049				
No 10	0.034				
No 11	0.026				
No 12	0.020				
No 13	0.012				

* Shots of 9s and below are all in the micro range

much of the weight should be concentrated in this position as happens when an Olivette is used. Various shapes of Olivette are available, the two principal ones being pear-shaped (known as Olivette Paquita and Olivette Torpille). There is also an oval one (known as Olivette Comte-Stix). In Fig. 34 examples of the former are on the right and the latter, on the left. The table gives the equivalent weight in English shot for Olivettes of the two main types. I have not included the oval Comte-Stix type as I have no use for them. In the pear-shape form, which I use all the time, I prefer the Paquita in sizes 1 − 12 and above that size, I go for the Torpille. All these leads have a central hole and it's through this that the line is passed when the lead is used to make up a particular tackle. When sold (see Fig. 34 again), the Olivettes have a wire fixed through the central hole. This is to prevent its small bore getting blocked and, for this reason, you should never remove the wire from an Olivette until you are actually going to put it on a line. Where the amount of weight needed is greater than the largest Olivette available (and this is an occasional rather than a regular need in pole fishing), I favour the ordinary barrel lead (Fig. 35) as used by pike anglers. I buy them in ½−2 in (1.2−5 cm) lengths and cut them to the size I need to cock a particular float. They cut easily, unlike an Olivette which is usually too hard to cut away.

Still on weight, you also need the kind of split shot you have always used. With rod and reel, the smallest size generally employed is dust shot. For the pole, you will also need micro shot and mini-micro shot, both of them smaller than dust. Advocates of continental (especially French) methods have advised a switch to some of the specialised weights they often use, instead of split shot. The two main types are mouse drop leads and Styl leads, the latter being small horizontal strips which have to be fixed to the line with a special tool. Because they feel that it is necessary to be copycats of the French, some English anglers have converted themselves to these leads and, it would seem, are fishing efficiently with them. I say they're not necessary.

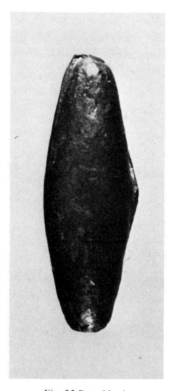

Fig. 35 Barrel lead.

There's quite enough to get used to in pole fishing without wishing yet another change on yourself, particularly when it will make no difference to your results. I have never used these leads and, equally, I have never come across any pole fishing situation where the normal English split shot cannot cope, always with the proviso that it's necessary to stock up on the small micro and mini-micro sizes. These latter, coupled with the diversity of floats I described earlier, are further evidence of the super-light sensitivity which can be achieved with the pole compared with rod and reel when the weight needed for casting is an extra consideration.

You will need elastics in the strengths I mentioned earlier, fine, medium, and strong.

69

As to line, again the pole permits you to get away with using much lighter line than you would employ with rod and reel. With the latter, I would guess that the lightest line most anglers would consider using would be a 1 lb (450 g) bs hook length. With the pole, you can go down to 12 oz (340 g) and 8 oz (226 g) with comfort and even 4 oz (113 g) though, personally, I would not use the latter. Doubtless, it's in these lighter gauges that the pole newcomer will need to add to his stocks. As to makes, everybody has his own favourites. For what it's worth, I use Maxima for all strengths from 2 lb (907 g) upwards and for anything less than 2 lb, Force.

Next, another important item — the hook. As a broad

Fig. 36 This excellent pole rod rest was designed specifically for pole fishing by Belgian anglers and is marketed by the Shakespeare Company. a) The pole is held securely in the rest by two circular clips at the rear. b) As soon as the pole is lifted, releasing pressure on the front support, the clips open.

generalisation, I would say that most match anglers in
England using the rod and reel think these days in terms of
hooks from 16s down to 22s. With the pole you can safely
go as small as a 24 or less. Some of my French friends go
as small as 28s! That, in my opinion, is too small for fishing
here and I merely mention it for interest, though I think
it worth adding that the reason they go so small is that
catching fish in France, especially in matches, is more
difficult than it is here. In England in most normal events,
an angler is mostly fishing to win individually and he would
never hope to succeed by catching the kind of tiddlers a
28 is designed to hook. The French, on the other hand,
fish very regularly in teams and a man catching tiddlers

71

in a bad section can still make a useful contribution to the outcome. Again, people always ask me what hooks I use for my pole fishing. These are the details: for maggot and caster for roach and small fish, VMC 9140 in sizes 16 to 24; for bloodworms, VMC Special Bloodworm hooks, 18s to 24s; for bread, caster, maggot and worm for bigger fish like bream, Mustad 39855 in sizes 10 to 22.

Finally, a series of small items of varying importance, the first of which is a plummet. It hardly needs mentioning except to emphasise that there is no form of fishing in which the *exact* use of a plummet is more important. You *must* plumb the depth with a plummet *without fail* every time you put a new tackle on the pole.

It's worth getting a pole rod rest (Fig. 36), but get it knowing that while you'll set it up every time you fish, you'll not be using it too often. The pole should never be fished from a rest. It should only be used when you need both hands for doing something else.

If you haven't got one, a bait stand which can be mounted on a bank stick is a good idea and, if your basket or box has not already got side trays mounted on it for holding bait, I'd say this was an essential addition.

Get these requirements sorted out and you'll be ready to start pole fishing in the next chapter.

4 Pole Methods for Still Water

We have now reached the stage where all the things I've been telling you about can be married together to create tackles that help you catch fish in all the situations in which a pole may be used. I have chosen to deal with still waters first because it's the best environment in which to start pole fishing as the tackles are simpler and also because most anglers find access to a local lake or pond easier than to rivers or canals.

In considering the first of our tackles, I shall describe how it is made up in considerable detail so that I may presume from here on you will realise that the method is the same for all the tackles which follow unless I make a reference to some basic difference.

Let's begin with what might be described as the classic pole tackle, for this shows clearly how the method works and how the other tackles follow on logically. We are going to fish at 5 m with the flick tip with a short line on the presumption that we are going to catch fish on the bottom of the lake.

The float to select is the balsa bristle (Fig. 26). The hook should be a 20 tied to a 1 lb (450 g) bs hook length of 12 in (30 cm). The main line – that's the line connecting the hook length to the pole tip – will be 1.5 lb (680 g) bs, the presumption being that it is a reasonably hard fished water and that the fish will not be all that easy to catch. Just how long the main line should be is the next important question. My experience tells me that, in general, the depth at most still waters at a range of 5 m is likely to be about

73

2 m so, let's work on that assumption. We want to fish maggot over depth which means the lowest 6 in (15 cm) of line will be on the bottom with the baited hook. This means that our line (including main line and hook length) must not be longer than 3 m in all.

Why? First to allow for the 60 cm between pole tip and float (we're fishing the short line method) before adding the distance between float and hook, ie 2 m plus the short length that is going to be laid on the bottom. From this, you can see that about 3 m is going to give us the correct length for the entire tackle (Fig. 37).

These dimensions settled, the next thing is to make sure that the Olivette and the small shot used to stop it dropping too far down the line (Fig. 37 again) are exactly balanced with the float so that when cocked just the white collar at the top of the float and the bristle are showing, a necessity which demands another digression.

Apart from presuming that you will make up all your pole tackles at home before fishing, one of the most important tasks is to ensure you get this balance just right. Using a bucket of water (Fig. 38) check this balance with different sized Olivettes until you get the display of float tip I've just described. With experience, of course, you develop a knack for selecting the right Olivette almost immediately. It follows, I hope, that once a particular Olivette and the additional shot and the float have been married together, they will remain together on a winder for use again and again without further checking. Once one of these tackles is balanced, it's balanced for good.

Equally, it should follow that *before* you do this balancing act, you have first fixed the float to the line by means of the eyelet ring at the top and the collar at the base. Next, withdraw the wire from the Olivette and thread it, with the thickest part down, onto the line. At first, you'll find that getting the Olivette on the line can be as tricky as threading a small needle. The tip, to make the job easier, is to trim the end of the line to be threaded by cutting it crosswise with a razor blade. Once the Olivette is on

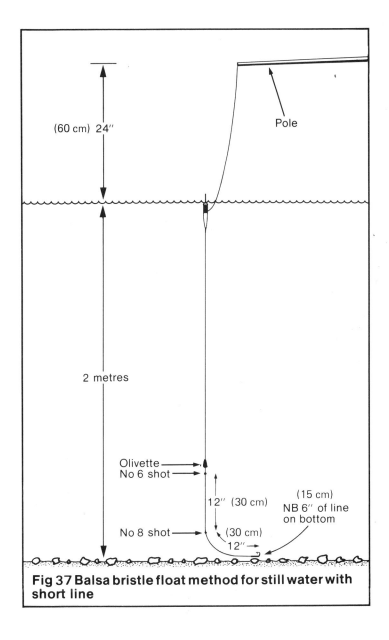

(60 cm) 24″

Pole

2 metres

Olivette
No 6 shot

12″ (30 cm)

(15 cm)
NB 6″ of line
on bottom

No 8 shot

(30 cm)
12″

Fig 37 Balsa bristle float method for still water with short line

Fig. 38 French international Guy Hébert balancing a pole float.

the line, you can add the other shots necessary to begin the task of balancing; in this instance a No 6 (the stop shot for the Olivette) and a No 8 (the latter to become the tell-tale for bites). With the float balanced you can then add the 20 hook on the 12 in (30 cm) hook length with a water knot (Fig. 39). Now put the float, shot and Olivette into their correct positions (Fig. 37 again) and wind the complete tackle onto its winder ready for use.

At the waterside, the tackle is simply unwound and the upper end of the line is tied to the loop on the pole tip

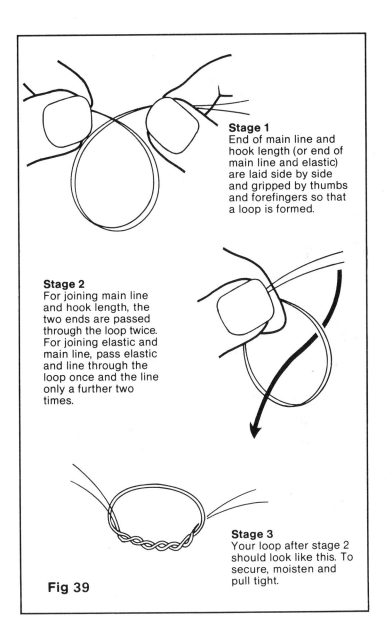

Stage 1
End of main line and hook length (or end of main line and elastic) are laid side by side and gripped by thumbs and forefingers so that a loop is formed.

Stage 2
For joining main line and hook length, the two ends are passed through the loop twice. For joining elastic and main line, pass elastic and line through the loop once and the line only a further two times.

Stage 3
Your loop after stage 2 should look like this. To secure, moisten and pull tight.

Fig 39

(Fig. 7). Before starting to fish, plumb the depth until you know the tackle is fishing as shown (Fig. 37 once more) with 6 in (15 cm) of line on the bottom but with the tell-table shot *suspended* . . . and we are ready for the off. Put a maggot on the hook and cast in and, as soon as the float has cocked, introduce some groundbait, stiffish in texture and laced with squatts or pinkies and a few maggots.

Hopefully, the float will dip reasonably quickly and, if you strike as I described earlier (Figs. 21 and 22), the fish should be cleanly hooked. As we are fishing at a range of 5 m with 3 m of line, it will be necessary to unship at least 2 m of pole (Fig. 23) before the fish can be swung to hand or brought to the landing net.

Let's say that bites slow or stop and you are beginning to wonder if the fish have gone. This might well be the case and a simple adjustment of the tackle is all you need to test this feeling. All you have to do (Fig. 37 once again) is move the tell-tale shot (the No 8) down the line until it's 6 in (15 cm) from the hook, at the same time moving the float 6 in (15 cm) up the line. This means we now have 12 in (30 cm) of line *and* the tell-tale shot on the bottom. In other words, we are fishing over depth.

Let's presume the fish respond once more with the tackle in this new position and suddenly you strike at one that was bigger than those you were catching previously and, worse still, it snaps your line. This, of course, is the situation which demands that elastic must be introduced into the tackle to prevent such a thing happening again. Replace the damaged hook length, make sure shots and Olivette are still in their correct position and wind the tackle back onto its winder.

If you've been as busy as you should have been at home, you will have another winder containing the same tackle ready made up, but incorporating 18 in (45 cm) of medium elastic, this strength being dictated by the 1 lb (450 g) bs hook length. The length of nylon in the previous tackle is reduced by 18 in (45 cm) to ensure that its 3 m total length remains unchanged despite the introduction of the elastic.

How should you have secured the elastic? Complete the tackle after balancing the float as described earlier. It is now necessary to secure the elastic to the main line before putting the tackle on its winder. To connect the elastic, lay the top end of the line and the lower end of the elastic, side by side and create a loop (as you would for the knot in Fig. 39). Pass the end of the elastic and the end of the nylon through the loop once. Then pass *the end of the line only* twice more through the same loop. Pull tight and you should have the neat join shown in Fig. 40. This knot is not only neat, it's also strong. If you've ended up with even the smallest loop after pulling the knot tight, start again for such loops can cause endless trouble if you attempt to fish with them. Now add a simple loop at the top of the elastic, this being used to fit that end of the tackle onto the winder and (Fig. 11) to the pole.

Back now to our still water. You have removed the rejected tackle and are about to fit its elasticated replacement. Before doing so, you must remove the flick tip from the pole and replace it with the separate top part fitted with the crook (Fig. 10) which will link the elastic (and the rest of the tackle) to the pole . . . and resume fishing.

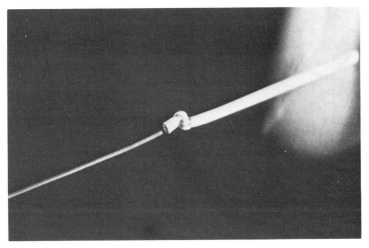

Fig. 40 Elastic and main line junction knot completed.

If I seem to have laboured the previous passage, this has been in the interests of pole-fishing newcomers. The change just described takes a matter of seconds — provided you always have the appropriate alternative tackle ready, and I shall presume from now on that not only will you have a good selection (Fig. 41), but it will not be necessary to repeat anything further about making this kind of change whilst fishing. One thing I do hope you noticed, however, is just how simple it is to change, and change again, once you have plenty of tackles made up.

Back on the lake once more we are fishing; the tackle with the elastic is now in position and instead of losing those better fish which are responding, we're getting them safely to the net — thanks, of course, to the shock-absorbing facility provided by the elastic.

Provided the conditions remain reasonable, this tackle

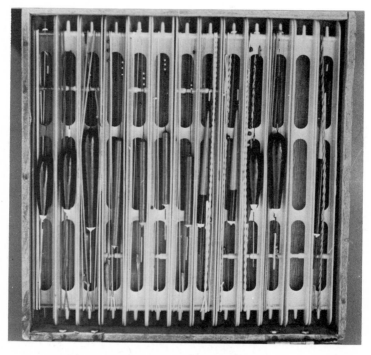

Fig. 41 A good selection of pole tackles on winders.

(with or without elastic) will serve in still water when you want to catch fish on or near the bottom; for each range you choose (ie from, say, 3−10 m) the same tackles will suffice, provided the depth remains the same. If the depth is greater (or less) a different tackle using the same float will be needed. The same is true if an alteration is desired in the strength of line or elastic, though the breaking strain of the hook length and the size of the hook itself can be changed without switching to a new tackle; but do remember to amend the code on the winder when you finish fishing with it. All this, I'm sure, is just further evidence as to how many tackles need to be prepared on your winders, if you are to stay versatile with your pole.

But what if the wind gets really strong? That is where you come up against a major limitation with the pole. It will become so difficult to hold, you will have to abandon it. Unfortunately the pole is no good in high winds. In such situations, the only way you can try and maintain contact with the fish is to switch to the rod and reel, with waggler float or leger.

From taking fish on the bottom, let's switch to the problem of fish going for the bait at all levels in still water, what is called 'on the drop'. An entirely different tackle is needed for this eventuality, and it's also the answer for when the surface is made choppy by the wind and an undertow develops. If you read carefully the last chapter, you should have already realised that the float needed now is the cocktail stick (Fig. 29).

This, you will recall, is the one I designed myself and which you will have to make if you wish to use it. In the circumstances I am about to describe, there is no other float I know that can compare with this one in still water.

To persuade you to share my feelings as to its importance, I'd like to tell you a little about how I came to develop it, for I'm sure this will help you understand better the need for its use.

Though I shall be telling you later about pole floats for canals, this float had its birth as a result of problems I was experiencing on canals. I was attempting to fish a short length of peacock quill fixed bottom only and there seemed no way on this particular occasion that I could get the float to stay upright and, thereby, fish correctly. Because of the top drag on the water, it would insist on leaning. It didn't *look* right and, as any of my friends will tell you, if I think anything in fishing doesn't look right I don't want to know about it because this suggests something is certainly wrong, even though one can't explain it. I decided that the answer was to add extra weight in some form to the base of the quill in the hope that this would make it cock vertically. That was when I jammed a cocktail stick into the base just to see what happened. I got the vertical 'show' I was looking for and, after a little bit of experimenting, the final design emerged. While the result did have application on canals, I went on to discover that in still water circumstances this float was beyond compare.

Look at the tackle (Fig. 42) before we discuss its merits. Immediately below the float is a No 6 shot. This gives it a self-cocking quality which is specially useful when fish are taking near the surface where they are always hard to catch. Unlike a deliberately made self-cocker, this float lands on the water with the minimum disturbance and so you are less likely to frighten the fish in this location where they are easily frightened. But don't think this float is just about catching surface feeders – far from it. The cocktail will catch fish at all depths, from just 6 in (15 cm) beneath the surface on down to the bottom. It has yet another advantage. It can be fished beyond the end of the pole, the method known as long lining which sees the distance between pole tip and float increased from the 24 in (60 cm), which is the limit for short lining which has the float directly under the pole tip. If you are fishing with a 5 m pole, this means that the float can be placed 3 m beyond the pole tip, the remaining 2 m of line covering the distance between the float and the bottom. This, I hope you will have noticed, brings yet another advantage. As we are fishing 5 m of line with a 5 m pole, it means the fish can be swung straight

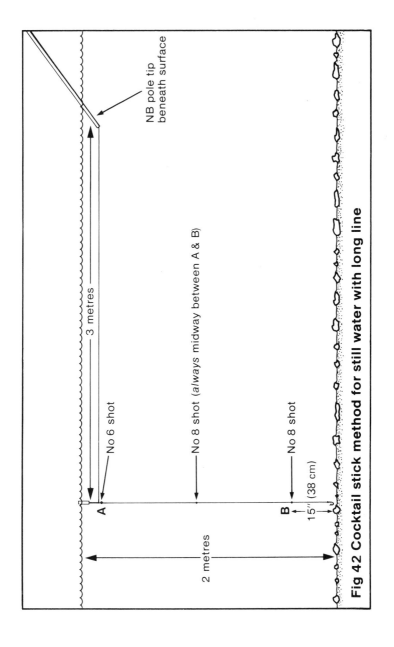

Fig 42 Cocktail stick method for still water with long line

NB pole tip beneath surface

3 metres

No 6 shot

No 8 shot (*always* midway between A & B)

No 8 shot

A

B

15" (38 cm)

2 metres

into your hand without any need to unship any sections of the pole. This, in turn, means that if fish are feeding keenly you can catch them faster. Notice the other shots, incidentally (Fig. 42 again). The shot between the float and the tell-tale is *always* placed exactly halfway between the other two.

To work most effectively, make sure after you have attached the complete tackle to the flick tip on the pole, that when it is suspended, the hook is at least 6 in (15 cm) above the butt of the pole otherwise when fish are swung in they will arrive *underneath* your hand, which is definitely not where you want them.

Consider yet another advantage. When you cast, the hookbait is 3 m beyond the pole tip, ie about 8 m from the bank. At that range, fish will take a bait more confidently near the surface than ever they would closer in. Remember, too, what I said when we were discussing the strike (Figs. 21 and 22). The strike with this method must *always* be a gentle sideways movement and *never* vertical. This is because fish taken like this generally swim off instantly with the bait. If you strike hard at such a fish, especially if it's any size, it will snap your line.

As I am sure you have realised I have a specially high regard for this tackle, not least because it helped me win six evening matches in a series of eight. In the other two, I was only beaten into second place because the winners had carp.

Like all tackles, this one is also subject to reservations. The first and most important is that the tackle must always be used with a flick tip and never with an elastic. If you look again at the diagram (Fig. 42 once more), you will notice that I have shown the tip of the pole buried beneath the surface. This is to enable you to keep the tightest possible line to the float from the pole while, at the same time, keeping this same length of line free from the effects of wind and surface drag. The introduction of an elastic would interfere with this to some extent but much worse is that it just doesn't seem possible to set the hook as accurately with elastic when used here. Many fish are lost because the elastic allows too much give at the instant of striking and so often prevents clean hooking. It could be argued that this failure to include an elastic could cost one bigger fish. Maybe, but the compensation is that you can still win a match with this method even if you do lose bigger fish because you catch so many if they are feeding.

Only one other thing needs saying about this tackle and that is what should be done if the wind strengthens. Do not deviate from the placements shown for the shot in the diagram, but increase them in size; ie instead of two No 8s and a No 6, use two No 6s and a No 4 or two No 4s and a No 1, the object being to make certain that you can still cast to the place where you were successful before the wind sprang up.

Though my French friends may disagree with me, the simple rigs I have described in this chapter are, in my opinion, *all* the pole angler needs for success on still water with all the normal baits *except* bloodworm. They are so simple I feel I must repeat what I said earlier – if you are a first-timer with the pole, choose this kind of water for your early lessons. There's so much less that can go wrong and that always makes for fast learning and greater confidence in what you are attempting.

Finally, I mentioned during the practicalities of fishing the balsa bristle the introduction of groundbait and the use of maggots. I propose to say no more at the moment for I feel the methods we have discussed are plenty to absorb in a single chapter. Later, I'll be giving you a comprehensive set of feeding patterns for use with these methods and those which follow for canals and rivers.

5 Pole Methods for Canals

Once upon a time, canals were not popular places to fish because they tended to have so few fish in them, thanks to pollution, abstraction, and a host of other causes of the kind anglers have been fighting for years to have improved. Those fish that were present were usually very difficult to catch. Latterly, however, the gloomy picture that was English canal fishing has changed for the better in many places. Nowhere, I suppose, is more typical than the Liverpool section of the Leeds and Liverpool Canal not far from my home in Leigh. It's so good now that the NFA are staging National Championships on it; this is after years during which the Federation was prevented from using canals for Championships after a special resolution had been passed at an NFA conference back in the 1960s. As a result of pressure from angling associations in the northwest, this decision has now been rescinded. A National Championship has also been staged on the Oxford Canal and, as I write, another is proposed using the Grand Union Canal. Thanks to the inspiration of these events, more matches are now being fished on canals and more and more anglers are fishing them, which means that it is more important than it was for a match angler to be equipped to fish them.

As all experienced match anglers will know, the rod and reel approaches we have used for so long can still be right for canals. This is specially true when the conditions are ideal and the fish willing and the place they can be caught is beyond the range of the longest pole. If, however, there's the slightest thing wrong with the conditions, that's the signal that the pole is the method to use, the finesse it offers being at its most useful when the fish are as shy as those found in so many of our canals.

It is amazing how often bites can be obtained from finicky fish like these, using the pole, when the same fish will not respond at all when tackled with rod and reel methods. Furthermore, I like to think I played something of a part in persuading anglers that on canals the pole really has come back to stay. It happened in a 400-peg event on the Leeds and Liverpool Canal, the *Liverpool Echo* Top Angler Open. I began this match with the rod and reel and was getting nowhere fast on a day when the canal had a strong pull on it, coupled with a downstream wind. Eventually, I found myself using a pole rig and the cocktail stick float, which I described in the last chapter, with the result that I won the match with 12 lb of roach and tench, doubling the weight of my nearest rival. To the best of my knowledge, that was the first match to be won with the pole on this canal in modern times and I did it with quality fish, too. I know it made quite an impression in tackle shops all over the north-west, for they were suddenly inundated by anglers wanting to buy poles! I am sure I need say no more to justify the pole in this setting.

On the barge canals, of which the Leeds and Liverpool and Grand Union are typical examples, it would be fair to say that while there are occasions when you will catch fish close to the near side with the pole at a length of only 3 m, most of the time the need seems to be to fish from the middle on across to the far side, a situation which means that pole fishing at 10 m is most often the norm. Whatever range you find you have to work — and only the peg you draw on the day can ever settle that — the rigs I am going to describe now are applicable at *whatever* range you need to fish.

With the aim of presenting these rigs in their most logical sequence, let's presume the conditions on the canal are ideal. There's little or no wind, but there might be a slight draw on the water. First thoughts would be that the match could still be won with rod and reel using a waggler float and that would be correct. So you start in this way and then certain things begin to happen . . . for instance, the fish seem obviously shy and, when you do get a bite, it seems distinctly chancey whether you will connect or not. As soon as that happens, or anything else which suggests that rod and reel fishing is not going to be plain sailing, then you must immediately begin to entertain thoughts of switching to the pole.

In the kind of ideal conditions we are considering at the moment, the best pole approach is with the gudgeon float, that's the one (Fig. 28) with the peacock quill body with a wire stem supporting it. Before describing the way the rig works (Fig. 43), two other points are worth making at this juncture. Notice first that this is the first time I have recommended using elastic threaded through the upper sections of the pole (Figs. 13 and 14) and this is because, on most canals these days, you can encounter the odd really big fish. In Lancashire, for instance, it could well be a sizable carp or tench, both being common at 3 lb (1.3 kg) or close to the maximum one could expect to subdue with a pole. Other canals have similar fish, hence this requirement. From this, you will not be surprised that my second point is that, on canals, you should *always* fish the elastic fixed in this way, for if used with a crook (Fig. 10), you will not have enough leeway with these better fish.

Now for the reasons why this rig is so good when you are trying to catch finicky fish in ideal conditions on a canal. Three adjectives say it all. It's light, sensitive and versatile. It could be fished just as it is but, on very hard days, it's the easiest thing in the world to give some 'life' to the bait with this rig. The first way of doing this is by lifting the pole to tease the bait by bringing it off the bottom and then letting it fall back. If there's a pull on the canal and the bait will not remain stationary and the fish want it still, you can achieve that stillness simply by holding the tackle back on a tight line with the pole.

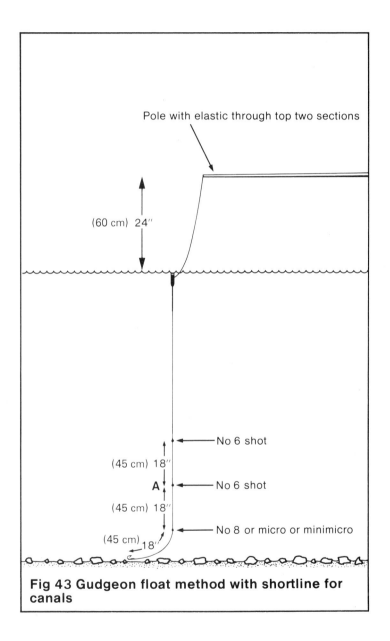

Pole with elastic through top two sections

(60 cm) 24″

No 6 shot

(45 cm) 18″

A No 6 shot

(45 cm) 18″

No 8 or micro or minimicro

(45 cm) 18″

Fig 43 Gudgeon float method with shortline for canals

Alternatively, you can make the bait move sideways in either an upstream or a downstream direction, again by moving the pole in the appropriate direction. Imparting movement to a bait with the pole like this is one of the first lessons we learnt from our continental friends, and a most valuable one it was, too.

It is truly remarkable how often one of these movements proves to be a positive fish catcher, and it's a lazy angler who chooses to fish this tackle in the same position all the time. Admittedly, this tactic works better with some baits than others. It can be an absolute killer with bloodworm and it's also good with maggot and caster, which is why the angler who uses this tackle with the pole will have a head start on the man who stays loyal to his rod and reel. I call it the 'kidder' because of the way it teases the fish into taking.

Look now at our diagram (Fig. 43 again). The lower shot will always be a No 8, a micro or minimicro; the shyer the fish, the smallest of these alternatives you use. Apart from teasing, it can often pay to move this tell-tale shot as close to the hook as 4 in (10 cm) another dodge that can be absolutely decisive. This is particularly effective on cold winter days, though that doesn't mean you shouldn't try it in the summer, too.

The only other point I want to make about this rig is that while the hookbait may be fished on the bottom (see Fig. 43 once more), it can also be laid firmly there, ie with the tell-tale on the deck as well as the hookbait, this being another change that can prove decisive. If the canal is pulling, however, you will have to use a bigger version of the float than the one shown in our diagram, because you will need to suspend the equivalent of three No 4s and, furthermore, these will be fished side by side as bulk shot at point A. When making this change, don't switch straight to No 4s. Try to get away with No 6s first, only changing to 4s if they are not enough. With rod and reel floats like wagglers, such a change in weight would be considered nothing of remark but, because everything about pole tackles is tied in with sensitivity, a decision to change just one shot (say a No 6 for a No 8) can make all the difference between catching and not catching, such is the dramatic effect a little adjustment can have on the efficiency of the tackle.

Once you get it right with this tackle, with the shots spread as in the diagram or bulked as I have just suggested, you will be astounded at the confidence of the bites you get. The float *and the line above it* will sail away under the surface and the fish don't seem to have a clue what is happening.

However, it won't need me to remind you that conditions on canals are far from always perfect and two such variations on a canal render the rig we have just been discussing useless. It then becomes necessary to change it again, both these circumstances being completely beyond the control of the rod and reel angler. The first of these changes is the crucial one. Instead of perfect conditions, the canal is flowing and the wind is blowing upstream in the opposite direction to the flow or, alternatively, a breeze strong enough to put a ripple on the water is blowing upstream though the canal itself remains stationary. To combat these circumstances, all you do (see Fig. 43 yet again) is to pinch a mini-micro shot onto the line above the float, which is known as a back shot. The object of this, as always with a back shot, is to increase your ability to sink the line out of the way of the wind and drag. If the canal starts moving *against* the wind, either by flowing or backing up, the float will automatically follow the flow against the wind. This means you are now using the elements themselves to give movement and life to the bait. Why a mini-micro? It's because the float is so small and well balanced already that anything heavier would sink the float.

The worst circumstance on a canal is when the wind is in the same direction as the flow — a downstreamer. It is now necessary to change to another float and your choice must be the dibber (Fig. 30), this being a piece of peacock quill with a cane insert in its base. As you can see (Fig. 44),

91

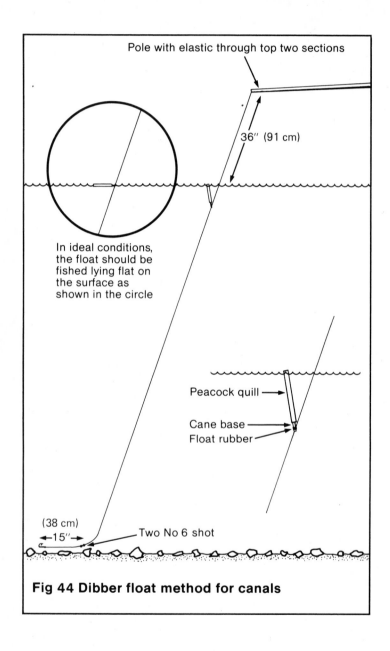

Pole with elastic through top two sections

36″ (91 cm)

In ideal conditions, the float should be fished lying flat on the surface as shown in the circle

Peacock quill

Cane base
Float rubber

(38 cm)
←15″→
Two No 6 shot

Fig 44 Dibber float method for canals

we are now laying the bait firmly on the deck, but we have done other things, as well. First of all, we are neither short-lining nor long-lining, the distance between float and pole being something in between, 36 in (91 cm). The reason for this is that in this kind of wind it is likely the pole itself will be moved from side to side, particularly if a long pole is being used. When this happens, it is essential to ensure that this movement does not also move the float on this rig. The extra length of line between float and pole is just enough to make certain that the line closest to the float is kept under the surface, something which, in my experience, would be impossible with a short line of 24 in (60 cm). Furthermore, if even 36 in (91 cm) is not enough for this to be done, a back shot (in this case a No 6) should be used to keep the line buried out of the way of the wind.

The next eventuality is when the wind becomes so strong, it drags the float in such a way that the shots will no longer keep the bait still on the bottom, which you must achieve all the time if this tackle is to work. The first answer is to change to a bigger dibber which will carry more shot. Try first two No 4s 15 in (38 cm) from the hook instead of the No 6s shown in our diagram. If that fails, the situation, believe me, is extreme and, as such, demands extreme measures to overcome it. It means that, for the first time in our tackle progression, we must resort to the float leger. Still using a dibber float, the set-up (Fig. 45) is as follows. The first thing to notice is that we now have a variable distance between the float and the pole tip. Previously, this was set at 36 in (91 cm), quite enough for the eventualities we discussed then. Now, however, the pole may be really swinging about in the wind and, if that is the case, you must increase this distance to 48 in (1.2 m) if you are to retain the ability to keep the line close to the float buried under the surface. Now look below the float and you will see that we have introduced a light paternoster. The single big shot is on a 9 in (22 cm) boom and the tail between the boom's junction with the main line and the hook is 3½ ft (1 m). Start with an AAA and, if that doesn't

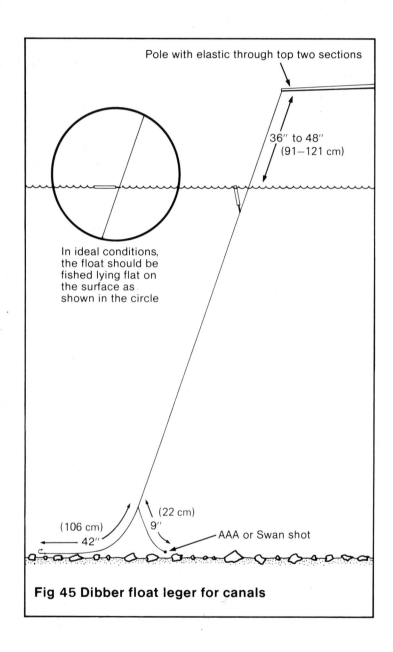

Pole with elastic through top two sections

36" to 48"
(91–121 cm)

In ideal conditions,
the float should be
fished lying flat on
the surface as
shown in the circle

(22 cm)
9"

(106 cm)
42"

AAA or Swan shot

Fig 45 Dibber float leger for canals

hold, change immediately to a swan. Bites will remain positive. It's just a question of doing everything you can to keep the pole itself under control in the strong wind.

These, then, are my pole tackles for canals when fishing baits like bread, caster, maggot and worm are used. I have one other rig which I use solely for bloodworms and this will be described in a special chapter devoted to fishing this bait with the pole. That exception made, all the rigs described in this chapter may be used as close as 3 m from the bank up to the maximum length of the pole available, though the longer the pole the more difficult it will become to retain control in more extreme conditions.

And now a final point about canals before we move on to the flowing rivers. Canals can often be clear and, in such water, fish can see the pole. Take a walk down a little frequented section of a clear canal and you will see the fish dive for cover. Walk down a piece which is regularly visited, particularly by anglers, and the fish are less cautious because they are more used to disturbance. Nevertheless, it's true to say that, initially, the pole can put fish off on a canal, this being more likely when a pole looms over a piece of water previously fished with a rod and reel. Don't worry about this. Just wait and, in a comparatively short time, the fish should get over the change. Furthermore, once you have got fish feeding keenly under the tip of a pole on a canal, it'll take a great deal of disturbance to put them down. The most important thing, of course, is that you must have confidence. I hope I need say no more to help in that direction.

6 Pole Methods for Flowing Rivers

Before considering the best pole fishing methods for these conditions, may I first of all draw your attention to the very deliberate use of the adjective 'flowing' in our chapter heading. This means I am going to be talking about rivers like the Severn, the Thames and the Trent, to name but three of the better known ones. That said, the question is immediately posed, what about the sluggish rivers, those like the Welland, the Witham, and the Nene which drain the Fenlands on the eastern side of the country? The answer, and I want to get this out of the way at the outset, is that on rivers like these (there are others apart from those in the Fens) is, in summer, to apply exactly the same rigs as those given in our chapter on still water in the same order. Later in the year, when rivers which were slow and sluggish in the summer can develop a definite flow, you apply the tackles which are to follow now. Turning to the rivers with real flow, I think it fair to say that, as far as pole fishing is concerned, they could well be described as those places where the pole is still facing the strongest resistance from the rod and reel anglers. After all, it's rivers like these that have been the basic attraction for generations of English anglers, the techniques which have developed have become so deeply ingrained in the minds of the anglers who fish them that they find it difficult, if not impossible, to consider using anything else. In float fishing, this faith is currently placed mostly in the stick float and the waggler. I am not criticising these methods. On their day, they are just the job but, as I have tried to demonstrate all through this book, there are more and more occasions now when the pole *does* have an English application, and flowing rivers are no exception. Those who have, so far, remained inflexible about this would be wise to give serious consideration to what is to follow.

Having said all this, however, it would be wrong if I did not immediately admit that the pole is *not* poised to take over *everywhere* on rivers like these. More and more places will come to be recognised as sections that respond to the pole approach while others will continue to be best tackled with rod and reel. Take the Severn as an example. There is no way in which the pole is ever going to become a worthwhile method on the upper reaches of this famous river. Yet, starting from Worcester and moving on down from what might be described as the lower middle reaches, I can see the pole being most successful. As I have said before, the Trent is one of our major match waters. These days, success on the Trent seems to have a cachet all of its own for those seeking a name in the match fishing game, the feeling being that the angler who has arrived here has arrived period. And yet it's my belief that this river, too, will become more and more fished with the pole, perhaps becoming the last great challenge in England for the acceptance of the technique. Though I am already convinced beyond doubt that the pole *will* win matches on the Trent, the vast majority of those currently centring their attentions on the river will be reluctant to give the pole a chance, for nowhere are old angling habits likely to take longer to die. So what should decide a man to give the pole a whirl on rivers like this? In my view, it's the kind of peg to be fished. The ideal pole peg on such a water would be stately in its flow and have a depth of about 8 ft (2.4 m), 5 m out from the bank, though the length of pole you would use to fish such a swim would be 9–10 m, a suggestion which should also tell you that you should only tackle this kind of swim with a pole when you feel you have acquired an advanced technique with it. Rivers like this are not places for pole fishing novices. Apart from this example there are other kinds of pegs on flowing rivers which justify the use of the pole, but I'd prefer to leave these until we get down to the actual detail of the rigs to use. In the meantime, I'd like to tell you about an experience I had on the Trent in the hope that it may convince you that excellent results can come from the pole, if only you try.

One of the main reasons why the pole has seemed ineffective on rivers like the Trent has been the swing to loose feed as the most positive method of seeking to concentrate fish in a swim. Groundbait has taken a back seat as it has come to be felt that in these waters, it is sudden death. From the pole angler's viewpoint, the wide spread over the swim achieved by loose feed makes it impossible to fish flowing rivers even with the longest pole. For the pole to work, a much more concentrated feed must be used, and that means groundbait or failure. As you will discover, I do not go for the sudden death theory about groundbait, which brings me to the experience I mentioned a moment ago. I went to the Ferry Field section of the Trent at Burton Joyce, near Nottingham, with my father to practise for a National Championship on the river. We both started fishing in the normal Trent style with wagglers about 15 m out from the bank. Both of us found ourselves struggling to catch. Eventually, my father switched to a swimfeeder and began picking up some nice, plump roach. That, I thought, was one method settled but what about the pole? Would it provide another useful answer? To put the idea to the test, I mixed some groundbait, about one-third medium-textured bread groundbait to two-thirds of fine soil taken from the river bank itself. Into this, I put a pint of casters and a sprinkling of maggots. Just like the continentals do in the five minute pre-baiting period which precedes the start of the World Championships, I banged in ten big balls on the 9 m line. I went in over it with the pole with maggot on a 20 under a big balsa bristle float (Fig. 26), balanced by a No 9 Olivette; the idea of this was to get the bait down quickly through the bleak, which were present, to the better fish I had hoped to line up below with that groundbait. In two hours, I had double figures in the net, a collection of sizable roach like my father's, three chub, and a carp of 1½ lb (680 g) — and I was broken five times by big fish I never saw even though I was using an elastic! The main point was that I had proved, to the particular surprise of my father, that groundbait was *not* taboo and that the pole would work as a method on the river.

The National Championship arrived and sadly I couldn't use the pole, for the peg I drew at Hoveringham was totally unsuited to it. It had to be fished with rod and reel if I was to stand any chance of notching a good points score for my team. Using the normal Trent approach, I had 15 lb (6.8 kg), mainly roach, and I won the section. It would have been a double thrill had I been able to do it with the pole.

As a result of experiences like this, the approach I have adopted on the Trent, and I hope many more experienced anglers will think it worth adopting the same attitude, is that whenever I draw a peg where I am certain I cannot win using rod and reel, then I will fish the pole. I have not yet won a match on this river in this way, but I do know of a number of matches that have been won by others using the pole. It's no secret, either, that the pole has been winning for some time on the Thames and, on the Severn, with bleak.

Another point worth mentioning here is that in the mid-1970s, when publicity for the pole began to escalate rapidly as a result of the ever-increasing interest being shown in the World Championships, there remained a nagging doubt in the minds of many that, basically, it was still just a method that worked with bloodworms and that, as such, it couldn't win matches except in the kind of canals found in Lancashire where this bait had long been used. Happily, this is another attitude that is changing. Anglers are winning matches in other places now with bloodworms, the most famous single example perhaps being the victory of Izaak

Walton (Preston) AA in the Division 2 National in 1976 on the River Witham in Lincolnshire. Every single man in the team fished bloodworm on the pole. That victory opened a lot of eyes and, since then, the bloodworm has become so successful at certain times on this river, some angling associations organising matches there decided to ban its use. Izaak Walton AA's win was absolutely no surprise to me for I had gained places in matches on the Witham with the bloodworm and the pole before they scored. Later, like them, I was to win with it, too, a development which brought further welcome publicity for the pole in the angling press.

And now another point which can be considered one of the most important you'll find in this book. In my early attempts to fish the pole on rivers, I decided, like so many others, to resist the rigs favoured by the continentals and sought to make English floats like the stick and the waggler work. There are still anglers trying to do this and, while they are catching some fish, they are simply leading themselves up a blind alley. I know. I tried the same thing and it was wrong. If you are going to fish the pole well, you must use the tackles that are specifically designed for it. They need not be slavish copies of those the continentals use, but based on their ideas, which, of course, as I said earlier, is now giving an English dimension to pole fishing.

Look now at our first pole rig for rivers (Fig. 46). It's for swims closely resembling the ideal I described earlier in this chapter, slow flowing and at least 2.4 m deep, 5 m out from the bank. Though it's similar to the balsa bristle rig I described for still water (Fig. 37), there are important differences. In this setting, elastic is a must. The distance between pole and float is 6 ft (1.8 m) instead of 2 ft (60 cm) and the hook is shown just touching bottom instead of laid on it. Let's examine the various differences in detail. And first, the question of balance. While you could get away with a little inaccuracy in the balance between the floats and the weight on still water, total accuracy is needed in this department on a river. That's

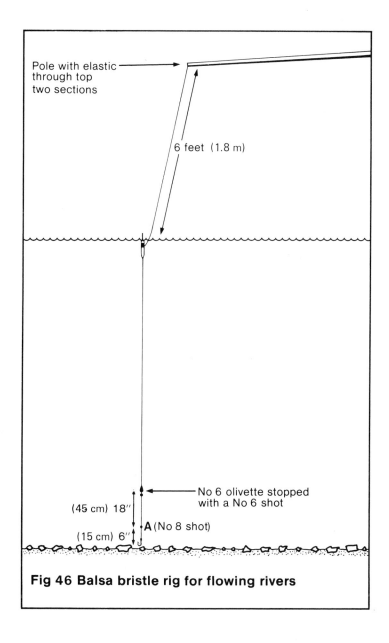

Pole with elastic
through top
two sections

6 feet (1.8 m)

No 6 olivette stopped
with a No 6 shot

(45 cm) 18"

A (No 8 shot)

(15 cm) 6"

Fig 46 Balsa bristle rig for flowing rivers

because the relationship between the Olivette and the tell-tale shot at point A is crucial on a river, and if you get it just slightly wrong the result will be fewer bites. Why is this so? Because you are using groundbait (the exact detail for feeding methods will be given in a later chapter), you are setting your stall out to catch fish on the bottom. The first consequence of this is that the Olivette will need to be fished closer to the hook, say an 18 in (45 cm) maximum instead of the 24 in (60 cm) specified for still water. And the same goes for the tell-tale at point A. In a river, the 6 in (15 cm) shown is your maximum. In still water, this was 12 in (30 cm). The second consequence is that if the tell-tale is not balanced it will have a tendency to be lifted off the bottom by the action of the float and current and so reduce the chance of the bait being taken by fish you have induced to feed on the deck with your groundbait. On page 67 I gave you a useful table giving you the comparative weights of Olivettes and our normal split shots. When I tell you I know it by heart, that's how valuable I consider it. As I said earlier, I use only the Paquita or Torpille patterns, depending on the amount of weight I require. A further qualification is that I would never use an Olivette smaller than a No 6 on a river, unless I was fishing for bleak or gudgeon; while continental anglers do regularly use the smaller Olivettes (sizes 1–4), I would not use them at all in this setting, preferring, as you will discover later, to use shots, either singly or in bulk. It should follow that you will not always be able to get your balsa bristle float to cock correctly with exactly the weights I have shown (ie a No 6 Olivette and No 8 shot). If extra weight is required to get this right, it should be added in the form of an additional shot immediately below the Olivette or by increasing (or decreasing) the size of the tell-tale shot.

Let's start fishing the rig now. The distances given for Olivette and tell-tale are ideal for putting the float through at the speed of the flow with the hook-bait just off or just touching the bottom. If bites develop immediately, that means fish are taking the bait freely on the run, which is exactly what the rig is designed to do. If they are not taking freely, the next gambit is to fish the bait harder on the bottom. To do this, move the tell-tale shot to a point 12 in (30 cm) from the hook. Leave the Olivette where it is at 18 in (45 cm) and move the float 6 in (15 cm) up the line. In this setting, the tackle may no longer be put through at the speed of flow. To do so would be to allow the tell-tale to catch on the deck and cause false bites on the float. To prevent this happening, the tackle must be held back with the pole just like one would do with a stick float with rod and reel.

But what if this change doesn't lead to any improvement, either? For this tackle, that's the point of no return. It's now necessary to change to another using a different float, which has attracted a great deal of publicity recently – the German design of float which I call the bung for the reason given in our accessories chapter. This float, which acquired its fame from the overwhelming victory scored by the West Germans in the 1981 World Championships in Germany with bream, is much misunderstood. It is, in fact, a one method float and yet anglers have been trying to make it do all sorts of things beyond its capability because it wasn't designed that way. That one method is your alternative when the balsa bristle pattern fails to deliver on flowing rivers, and this is the *only* use you should make of this float.

Look now at the diagram (Fig. 47). Almost immediately above the hook are three No 6 shot in three positions on the bottom, each being kept there by holding the pole hard back while putting the tackle through the swim – laying on on the move. The Olivette is the Torpille pattern and this is the only tackle for which I use this type. It is still pear-shaped but not as accurately pear-shaped as the Paquita. It has the advantage that it has a bigger hole through the middle and this allows you to stop it on the line by inserting a short piece of thin bristle as a stopper instead of doing this with a shot. Why do this? It's because these leads (the smallest to be used for this purpose being

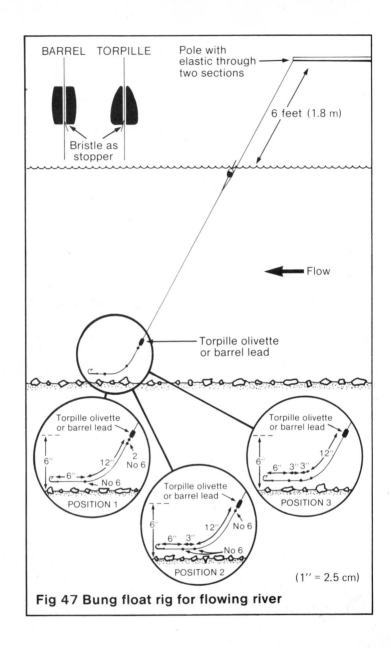

Fig 47 Bung float rig for flowing river

3.5 g), if allowed to move up and down like a freely threaded Olivette, are so heavy they can damage the shot down near the hook. By securing it with a piece of bristle you ensure it stays put, though you are still able to change its position if desired by sliding it up and down the line with the bristle in place. If you prefer it for easier working, you can use the sort of barrel lead used by pike anglers (Fig. 35). The beauty of these is that not only do they do the same job, but they are soft enough to be easily cut whenever you require a slight adjustment in size. They are still held in position the same way, by a bristle. For barrels, it should be a fairly strong bristle from something like a yard broom.

This tricky float will only work correctly if it is fished with a great deal of accuracy, held back and literally inched down the swim; it's the failure to do this properly that has led so many anglers to get into difficulties. The first and most important thing to understand is that whichever of the three positions in our diagram you eventually find yourself using (see Fig. 47 again, positions 1, 2, and 3), the Olivette (or barrel lead) must *always* be fished not more than 6 in (15 cm) from the bottom, this being vital to ensure that the bait fishes on the deck and is not swung up from it by the flow. Notice, too, that I have specified a distance of 6 ft (1.8 m) from pole tip to float, the reason for this being to permit the maximum possible distance in your swim. It gives you a longer trot.

Of the three positions shown for the end tackle, the one to try first is No 1 because if you can get away with just the single No 6 shown on the bottom in this way, the float will be working at its most efficient. If, having done this, you contact fish quickly then there is no need to make any further alteration. Once the tackle is in the water and the float cocked so that just the antenna shows, inch the tackle down the swim, holding it back with the pole. Then hold it dead still for a minute or two and, if a bite doesn't result from that, induce it to move on before stopping it once more, repeating this stop-start form of presentation as far as the pole will permit.

If bites don't result with the end tackle set as in position No 1, change the setting to that shown in position 2 and, of course, if that doesn't produce, work finally to the shotting pattern in position 3, remembering that whichever position is being used that Olivette must *never* be more than 6 in (15 cm) from the bottom.

Now if that sounds simple, you are right, it is. As always in most angling situations, however, there can be complications. With this float, the main one is that fish can strip the bait from the hook and yet the float hasn't registered the bite quickly enough for you to connect. With this float, you mostly don't even see these bites. You just discover a ragged bait when the tackle is recovered for the next swim down the peg. Obviously, you want to do something to try and stop any more baits being stripped like this. The reason it's happening adds up to the need for the reverse procedure to the one I have just described where we put more and more shot on the bottom to combat the effect of a stronger current. When bait stripping develops with this rig, it's because the bait is now being fished *too hard* on the bottom and, therefore, it is now necessary to work back through the positions, reducing the number of shot on the bottom, until, hopefully, bait stripping ceases and the fish are being cleanly hooked once more.

Still emphasising that this is a very specialised method, let me remind you of what I said when I described these floats earlier in this book. They were designed by the Germans to catch bream and are definitely most successful when these fish are the quarry. They also work well for other big fish, like sizable roach and chub. Problems usually develop when you find yourself attempting to catch smaller roach and dace with the tackle. When that happens, you have to tell yourself that you are now in a legering situation, by which I mean that when you are legering you never expect to hit every bite. Nobody ever does. You must accept that you *will* miss bites with this rig when smaller fish are about, and simply content yourself with the feeling that at least you are catching your share.

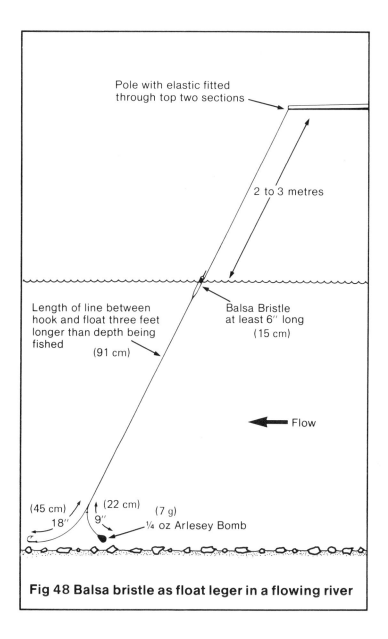

Pole with elastic fitted
through top two sections

2 to 3 metres

Length of line between
hook and float three feet
longer than depth being
fished
(91 cm)

Balsa Bristle
at least 6″ long
(15 cm)

Flow

(45 cm)   (22 cm)   (7 g)
   18″   9″   ¼ oz Arlesey Bomb

Fig 48 Balsa bristle as float leger in a flowing river

Let us now presume the bung has brought you no bites despite progressing through the various stages I have outlined. It can happen. What should you try next with your pole? The only answer is to switch to the float leger (Fig. 48). This is what I call the odd fish rig. In other words, it may catch you one or two bonus fish or nothing. It can also be described as an improved version of the float leger I suggested for canals (Fig. 45). It is important to set this rig up exactly right if you are to get any benefit from it. Perhaps the most vital thing of all is to ensure that the amount of line between hook and float is 3 ft (91 cm) longer than the depth of water being fished, ie in 6 ft (1.8 m) of water this distance would be 9 ft (2.7 m) and pro rata. The rest of the rig is self-explanatory, except to direct your attention to the fact that the length of line recommended between pole tip and float is the longest yet specified. There are two reasons for this. The first is that, because of the flow, the fish have dropped further down the swim and you need to be able to reach that far with your hookbait. The second is that if you don't make this provision in the powerful flow you are fishing, the float will tend to vibrate constantly and even give false bites. The variation is between 2 and 3 m for this part of the line. The deeper the water the shorter this distance should be, the shallower, the longer.

To conclude this chapter, I would simply say that if the tackles outlined do not produce results there is no other pole rig that will catch you fish in a flowing river and you must resort to conventional English float tackles or leger with the quivertip or swimfeeder.

7 Feeding Methods for the Pole

Having told you how to fish still waters, canals and rivers with the pole, I'm going to switch now to telling you how to compliment those methods with feeding patterns that will actually catch the fish, the one being useless without the other. Only by feeding correctly for each method can we ever hope to get the kind of response we want from the fish.

Before I link these patterns to the various kinds of water, there are several general points worth making.

First, every pole angler *must* learn how to feed with one hand. This means that if you are right-handed, you must be able to feed with your left and vice versa. If you don't do this, you will be putting your pole down constantly or changing it from hand to hand, thus costing yourself valuable fishing time (especially in a match) or risking a missed bite. I would accept that this is not a factor if you are using a short pole for, obviously, you can simply change hands with this while you feed, but you cannot do that with a long pole and this is why I recommend that you get into the habit from the start of feeding with the hand you are not used to using. You will be a much more efficient pole angler if you train yourself to do this whatever length of pole is in use.

You will be surprised if you are a newcomer just how cumbersome a long pole will feel at first, even if it's made of carbon fibre and you will only get the benefit of this seemingly ungainly tool by developing ease of handling. I think it is equally essential not only to be able to feed groundbait while holding the pole but, also loose feed, either by hand or catapult, while still supporting the pole with the hookbait retained in a takeable position.

There are two stances you can use. The first (Fig. 49) demands that you place the butt of the pole across the top of the thigh and trap it by pressing your stomach on it. This allows you to take *both* hands off the pole to use your catapult. If you were feeding by hand only, you would simply support the pole with one hand while feeding with the other (Fig. 50). Another alternative is to have a hook on a telescopic support on the rear of your basket or box. The butt of the pole is trapped under the hook, with the pole supported on the thigh, again leaving both hands free. The other advantage of this hook is that during periods of inactivity, it can be used as a constant support

Fig. 49 Trapping the pole with stomach leaving both hands free for the catapult.

110

Fig. 50 Feeding with one hand. Notice the maggot box and groundbait tray in easy reach.

for the pole leaving one hand free all the time, a specially welcome facility in winter conditions.

While you would think nothing of putting your rod in a rest when fishing with rod and reel, very few pole anglers I know do this because of the time it takes to fit the pole carefully into the rests (Fig. 36) and to take it out. The only thing in favour of the pole in a rest is that it gives you a reasonable guarantee in terms of fixing the feeding point at or near the pole tip.

Equally important is that the pole angler must be much more tidy in how he sets out his stall than the rod and reel angler *before* he starts fishing. The French are so fussy about this, it's common to see plan drawings of well-known

111

anglers' pegs showing just how they set things out. While that's going a little too far, it is necessary to have everything to hand because the degree of movement one has while fishing the pole is much less than with rod and reel. This is why I think it essential to have trays fitted on the side of your basket but, as an alternative, you can use a bait tray mounted on a bank stick or placed handily on top of some piece of equipment you are not using.

The side tray on the basket is used for loose feed like maggots or casters while, for easy working, the groundbait bowl is placed to the rear or immediately to the side of the bait tray, thus ensuring that both kinds of feed are available for throwing with one hand.

Generalisations complete, let's move to our detailed feeding patterns on the understanding that all those re-lating to bloodworm will be dealt with in a separate chapter.

First, feeding patterns for still water. Here, as with any type of water, three factors decide what an angler's attitude to feeding should be: the species likely to be caught, the stamp of fish likely to be encountered and the numbers present.

Let's now link these with feeding patterns for the balsa bristle method shown in Fig. 37. Let's say the likely fish are roach and skimmer bream to 4 oz (113 g). The hook-bait will be maggot on a 20 with a short line between pole and float. Medium texture bread groundbait should be mixed with squatts or pinkies. Begin by introducing two or three small balls of a size that could be clenched in one hand. After 15 minutes, you start catching. If the likely winning weight in the match you are fishing is 5 lb (2.2 kg) add another ball of feed for every three fish caught. If, however, a bigger weight is on the cards and the fish are responding well, especially the skimmers, add a ball of feed for every fish caught. Consider the converse. Either bites didn't develop or, after catching, they stopped. Cut back the rate of feed and start presuming that there are not as many fish present in your swim as you thought. If bites still don't develop, mix some fresh groundbait of the fine texture that will cloud in the water. Put in one walnut-sized piece only. If this is the answer, the fish will respond again in a matter of minutes. If it's not, abandon any idea of using any more groundbait, but keep giving them a light sprinkling of loose feed. You have now reached the point of no return. You simply accept that loose feed is all you dare use until the end of the match, resigned to the fact that this was one day when you drew a bad peg!

Now the same bristle float rig in a water where, in addition to small stuff, there are bigger fish, roach, bream and, possibly, tench. If the water is one you don't know, start as just described for small fish until you discover the presence of their bigger brothers. Once that happens the groundbait mix should be changed so that it's mainly laced with casters (though still including a few squatts or maggots) with maggot still on the hook. If you knew the water in advance, you would use this mix from the start. Feed to the same sequence as before but keep trying caster as an alternative bait on the hook. The main problem with bigger fish is that all too often they don't like lumps of groundbait cascading down through the water onto their heads, this being specially true at close range. If you feel that this kind of resistance is developing, forget the groundbait, and loose feed caster or maggot, the choice depending on which is the positive hookbait. Whichever hookbait you are using, it always pays to accept that casters as feed are more likely to bring bigger fish.

Another feed alternative to consider if sizable fish are responding is hempseed, loose fed with caster and caster on the hook. Begin by putting down a carpet of hempseed round the hookbait (say two handfuls). Follow through by loose feeding caster onto this carpet. If it works, bites will come. If they slow, more hemp rather than caster should regain the fish's interest.

A final alternative with the balsa bristle in still water is to consider using hemp on its own, a decision you could take if only you know the water. The loose hemp would be introduced sparingly at regular intervals on the little and often principle, with hemp the positive hookbait.

Now the feeding pattern for the cocktail float in still water as described in Fig. 42. Presume that it is unlikely that roach, hybrids and skimmers are present with big fish. My first feeding pattern works best in the early season when, as every angler knows, fish are more willing to take our offerings. For obvious reasons, it's also designed to tempt fish at all levels, something which should immediately tell you that it involves loose feed only. Whether this will be maggot or caster will again depend on advance know-ledge of the water or, if not, discovering during the early stages which is the more positive. Our aim must be to ensure that there are loose samples of the bait trickling down through the water *at all levels all the time*, which means your hand will be in the bait box very regularly indeed. It offers a special reward for those who taught themselves to feed one-handed. A fair yardstick would be to throw six maggots (or casters) every minute, increasing this rate if bites come so quickly they suggest the fish want more. Indeed, if all goes well it could lead to constant feed-ing coupled, if you're doing really well, with an increase to a couple of dozen samples every throw. If, however, they don't come quickly, stick to the rate of six samples a minute. Presume now that after a period of catching on the drop, the fish are not showing an interest in the bait at all levels and those we are still picking up are tending to take near the bottom, a situation which often develops after a period of successful drop fishing. The trick now is to fish on with the same tackle but cut the loose feed back to no more than six samples a minute. While we were drop fishing, the bait was retrieved the moment it reached its maximum depth, and re-cast, to make sure that the hook-bait, like the loose samples, was always falling down through the water. In this new situation, we let the hook-bait reach its maximum depth and leave it there because the feeding fish are now at the lower levels, thanks to all the loose feed that has collected there. It follows that as you are now denying them the generous quantities of loose feed, the fish, if still present, will begin to rise again in the water. When this happens, you increase the loose feed once more and, hopefully, start catching them on the drop again. Indeed, in the course of a match you could be switching constantly in the way I have described to retain contact, at the same time changing the feeding pattern to match. The same feeding pattern is also very good when a wind springs up and creates an undertow which is flowing in the opposite direction to the wind. When this happens, we say the float is 'tripping up' against the wind. The only other point I would make about this drop feeding system just described is that it can also pay if you throw occasional walnut-sized pieces of cloud groundbait. On waters where there are a lot of fish present, you can make this offering regular, rather than occasional, with safety.

And that completes the feeding patterns for still waters. Let's move on now to canals with first, fishing the gudgeon float (Fig. 43), when roach, bream, skimmers, tench and, perhaps, the occasional carp may result. Start at 9 in (22 cm) with caster on an 18 hook with the tackle set so that the tell-tale shot is just off bottom with the last 6 in (15 cm) of line lying on the deck itself. Loose feed from the start with a catapult because of the range you're fishing. Begin with two good pouches of hempseed and follow through immediately with two more of caster. Generally, it's likely to be at least 15 minutes before you get your first bite. If that happens, catch at least three fish before you give them another dozen casters. If fish keep coming, shoot another pouch after every fish from now on. If you have drawn a good peg, this pattern could continue right through to the end of the match. If this has brought you two dozen fish, you must be in the money on a canal, for this caster method usually attracts quality fish. If after catching, the sequence starts to fall apart, put in two more pouches of hemp and two of casters and, as you did at the start, sit on it for 15 minutes in the hope that catching will resume. But what if you didn't catch after the first 15 minutes and time is passing with no result? Increase the amount of line laying on the bottom with the tell-tale shot also on the deck. If that doesn't produce a response, take it from me you are going to struggle. Simply play a waiting game, putting in a few casters at intervals of not less than half-an-hour. And while you are waiting, remember that as a weight of 5 lb (2.2 kg) is enough to win most canal matches, a match fished like the waiting game you are playing could still be won in the last hour, so don't despair. The secret is not to be tempted to exceed that 30-minute feed interval until it's clear there has been a positive change of attitude downstairs. What if you want the hookbait in this setting to be maggot? Simply substitute maggot for caster in the sequence just described, eliminating hemp-seed entirely from your offerings.

Now consider the same float with small fish the likely outcome, say roach and skimmers. Offer maggot on a 20. Mix some cloud groundbait laced with squatts or pinkies. Introduce two small balls of this at 9 m. If fish respond, put in another ball as each fish is caught. If the response is slow, play a waiting game, reducing the feeding interval as before.

Now the dibber float on canals as discussed for Fig. 44. The feeding patterns for this float are the same as those just given for the gudgeon float, depending on the kind of fish likely to be encountered and the hookbait being used. So why change to this float? There are two reasons. The first is that the fish want the bait harder on the bottom than can be achieved with the gudgeon float (ie as much as 18 in (45 cm) to 3 ft (91 cm) of the line immediately above the hook on the deck). It is also better than the gudgeon float if a wind sprang up. Finally on canals, the dibber as float leger (Fig. 45). Again, the same feeding patterns can be applied as desired.

And now, feeding patterns for pole fishing on flowing rivers with first the balsa bristle as shown in Fig. 46. Presume all the usual species in all sizes could respond. First, what I call the caster method. Use an 8 m pole with

6 ft (1.8 m) of line between pole tip and float with caster on an 18. If the flow is not too fast for loose feed (ie you are sure it will get to the bottom within one or two metres of the point at which it is introduced), then go for loose feed. Begin with two handfuls of casters and two of hempseed. If fish respond, continue to feed with caster *and* hemp mixed together. Keep this up in step with the bites. If they continue, keep the feed going. If they slow, slacken off the feed. If the flow is too fast to get loose feed to the bottom in the distance stated, use groundbait. If the water is one where you know the fish will take groundbait anyway, forget loose feed and use groundbait from the start. Begin with two balls of groundbait and continue to feed in sequence with bites. Early season, it pays to put this float through with the speed of the water when fishing to this feeding pattern, while maintaining a reasonably tight line between pole tip and float. As the season progresses, you will find it more and more likely that you will need to hold the float back as this can often make all the difference. If maggot is to be the positive bait, offer it on a 20. Eliminate the hempseed from the pattern and do *not* use groundbait. For reasons I cannot explain, fish just don't seem to take maggot these days when groundbait is used. So with this method, it's loose feed if it'll hit bottom in one to two metres. But what if the flow means it can't? How do we proceed now when the usual alternative for meeting this situation, groundbait, is going to upset the fish? The answer is to use a bait dropper (Fig. 51) to get loose maggots where you want them. The bait dropper is packed with maggots which are released by a weighted lever when it strikes the river bed, preferably at the head of the swim. The best way to use a dropper is to fix it to a spare pole of exactly the same length as the one on which you are fishing. Not only is time saved, great accuracy is achieved in the placing of the feed. If you haven't got a spare pole then you can insert the hook into the corks fixed to the bait dropper which can be seen in our illustration. As a bait dropper holds so many maggots, it's easy

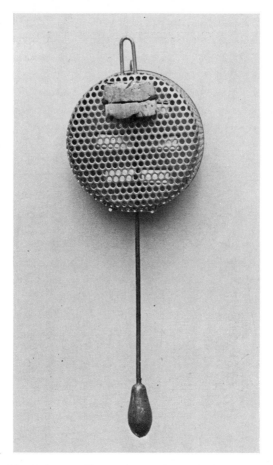

Fig. 51 Bait dropper. Note corks near the top for fixing the hook.

to overdo the amount of feed. The sequence I find best is to put in a full dropper at the start and repeat the dose every 15 to 20 minutes thereafter. At the same time, it's a good thing to feed a few loose maggots every so often. Even though they will not get down to the bottom within range of your pole because of the speed of the flow, they will serve to draw the fish downstream towards the place where you want them.

Now that tricky float to operate, the bung (Fig. 47). In

118

fact, the feeding patterns are exactly the same as for the balsa bristle in all those instances where loose feed or groundbait can be got to the bottom within one or two metres of the point of introduction. If, however, you are forced to use a bait dropper, this should be used with samples of the hookbait being used. Previously, it was cited only as an aid for maggots but other baits, like caster, can be fed through the dropper in strong flows. Exactly the same comments go for the balsa bristle in the float leger situation (Fig. 48).

Experienced anglers will be well acquainted with these feeding patterns. Newcomers to the sport, however, should not presume they are for use *solely* with the pole. All of them are perfectly valid for use with rod and reel in the settings described. I'd simply add that it is *always* better to underdo it with feed than vice versa. Once more feed has been introduced into any swim than the fish will accept, it's very very difficult to repair the damage. You must balance the supply and the demand as exactly as possible so that the fish get just enough to keep them interested. While you have given them the main course, they must still be waiting for desert when you are packing up. It is equally true to say feeding of some kind is usually necessary, without it, you won't catch, except for those rare circumstances on very hard waters in winter where any feed might be fatal.

Finally in this chapter, I'd like to refer to the many exotic continental feeds now being offered on the English market. At this moment, I feel it is too early to say anything categorical as to their effectiveness, though I know many of the better French anglers are fans of the mixture known as Amorces Tesse, which is named after France's best known match angler. Certainly the mixtures in this chapter will do all that is necessary in England at the moment. I shall, of course, be trying these French mixes but, as I have said about the pole method in general, it could well turn out to be another instance when it may not be a good thing to follow the lead of our continental friends too closely. Those who want more information about continental bait mixes should consult *The Encyclopaedia of Coarse Fishing Baits* by Colin Graham (Macdonald and Janes). It contains more information on this subject than any other book I know.

8 The Pole and Bloodworm

When the pole first began to attract the attention of English anglers as a result of the World Championships, many dismissed it as a one-bait method. That bait was the bloodworm, which is considered the number one bait with continental anglers like the French and Belgians. It was doubly dismissed when most people, including myself, expressed the view that while bloodworm might be all right on the continent, it couldn't win matches in this country. Both these assertions, I submit, have since been proved completely false. The pole, as we have seen in earlier chapters, works well with all the baits we have been familiar with for so long. And, of course, bloodworm *does* win matches here now. Whatever your feeling about the current state of these arguments, there is not the slightest doubt whatsoever that the pole is not only a superb method when it comes to fishing bloodworm, it's infinitely superior for this purpose than the rod and reel. The reason for this is simple. The bloodworm is a delicate bait which demands equally delicate presentation. The pole fulfils that need to perfection. Certainly no thinking English match angler can now afford to ignore this trend, which is why I decided to devote an entire chapter to what I feel is one of the most important aspects of pole fishing.

Of the floats discussed so far in this book, three are relevant to fishing the bloodworm, the balsa bristle (Fig. 26), the cocktail stick (Fig. 29), and the gudgeon float (Fig. 28) together with a fourth, the bodied bristle (Fig. 27). How do these floats fit into the type of waters to be fished when bloodworm is the bait? On still waters and canals, four of them, the balsa bristle, the cocktail, the gudgeon and the bodied bristle, are likely to be needed. On rivers, only two, the balsa bristle and bodied bristle, are relevant.

A good generalisation at this stage would be to say that all lines and hooks will need to be finer for bloodworm fishing than for the baits discussed earlier. It's equally true to say that this bait is at its most successful when it's fished *just* off the bottom or *just* touching it.

Now before we go any further, I don't intend telling you how to get bloodworms and jokers, the latter being the smaller, more active form of bloodworm which are used as feeders. Enough has been written on this subject elsewhere and the angler who is really keen will already have obtained the necessary information. For those still in the dark, the fullest guide is again contained in *The Encyclopaedia of Coarse Fishing Baits* by Colin Graham (Macdonald and Janes). Not so readily available is accurate information as to how to fish the bloodworm and it's that omission I hope to deal with in this chapter. As before, I think it will be best assimilated by a progression through the various types of water in the same order as before, which means we begin with still waters.

The first float relevant here with the pole and blood-worm is the balsa bristle (Fig. 26). For starters, this, without question, is the classic bloodworm float, designed for fishing the bait at long range by the continental anglers who created it. Now while bloodworm is most effective in this setting at a range of 10 m where it will take big and small fish, this float will also fish the bait well at ranges down to 5 m. Nevertheless, there's no doubt in my mind that a big catch is more likely with it at 10 m simply because, as we have seen earlier, the better fish tend to keep their distance from the shore.

And now the balsa bristle methods for still water (Fig. 37). Presume the range is 10 m (but it can be less if you wish). Instead of the 24 in (60 cm) I specified for the distance between pole and float in this diagram, this distance should now be reduced to 18 in (45 cm), the shortest short line specified so far. The bloodworm should be offered on a 22 hook tied to a 1 lb (450 g) hook length which, in turn, is linked to a 1½ lb (680 g) main line. The appropriate elastic is *essential* and should be of the type fitted through the top two sections of the pole and *not* fished with a crook (Figs. 13 and 14). The feed is made up of 50 per cent finely riddled soil and 50 per cent fine textured bread groundbait. This should be mixed with water until just damp so that it will hold together easily when clenched in the hand. Raw bloodworms should be laced in at the last moment, a good yardstick for quantity being that if you expect to catch double figures the amount should be at least a litre. Notice particularly that I said raw bloodworms in the mix and *not* the smaller jokers normally associated when feeding with bloodworm on the hook. Where quality fish are concerned, and they're what we're hoping to catch in this instance, I have found from experience that you are more likely to catch them if you use bloodworms on the hook *and* in the feed.

The most important thing when feeding with bloodworms is that the bait must be introduced into the swim with much greater accuracy than is needed when other hookbaits are being fished and, what's more, the pole helps you to pinpoint the placing of the feed much better than any other tackle. Before beginning to feed, place the pole in its rest so that you can discover *exactly* where in the water the tip will be when fishing. With the pole still in the rest, put ten balls of your feed into the water within an imaginary circle 18 in (45 cm) in diameter round the pole tip, really tight, accurate feeding. At one time, of course, many English anglers were amazed when they heard of the way in which the continentals put in such large amounts of feed at the outset when bloodworm fishing. They considered it sacrilege and bound to frighten off every fish within miles. It's one more prejudice which has been knocked into a new perspective by the increasing use of pole and bloodworm in this country. I well remember, in fact, the first time I did this on the Kirkstead match length of the River Witham in Lincolnshire in the early 1970s. The angler at the next peg not only remonstrated with me, he accused me of lifting the river level, two feet (60 cm). He had changed his tune by the end of the match when I finished with second place and double figures, while he had felt obliged to pack his tackle and go some time before the finish.

So, we have put in our feed using the pole itself as our guide. Go in now with the baited hook on top of the feed, remembering that it should be on or just off bottom but never laid on. If you are going to have a good catch, I'll wager that the first bite comes within five minutes. If that happens, there is no need to introduce any more feed unless bites slacken or stop. Such an initial feed as I have described should catch at least 50 fish. If the fish do go off after an initial burst of success, don't go putting in another ten balls of feed. Introduce this follow-up feed in walnut-sized balls on the little and reasonably often principle. If you don't catch within five minutes of the initial feed being introduced, you can consider that this is one day when you may well not catch, or that the method must be changed to the next one we are to discuss. Meanwhile, I'm sure you would agree that the method I have just outlined couldn't be simpler and why it's been surrounded with so much mystery by some is beyond me.

For that next method for bloodworm, we must change to the cocktail stick float (Fig. 29), now with a flick tip top on the pole and no elastic. I hope you will have remembered that this float was designed to take fish at all levels in the water, which is what you must attempt when it's clear that your bloodworms are not being taken on the bottom. When it does work with bloodworm, my experience tells me that the result will be perch and small fish only, still perfectly acceptable if they are going to win you a match. Furthermore, if advance knowledge tells you this could be the winning method from the start then this is the one you would go for from the start, with 5 m the likeliest range at which to succeed with it. You would also make sure there was a fairly long line between pole and float so that once you've taken the depth into account the small fish can be lifted and swung directly to your hand. Again, I would emphasise that the bait should be just on or off the bottom. The bloodworm should be fished on a 22 hook (Fig. 52), with a No 6, set 12 in (30 cm) from the hook with two more No 6s pinched on just below the float to give it a self-cocking effect, all this suggesting that we are very definitely fishing in the top layers of the water at the start. And now for the all important feed. Take some fine black garden peat (any coarse bits should be riddled out) and put this in your bait mixing bowl. Now add jokers, these being most necessary with this technique. Don't mix all the jokers in at once. Just add some to the peat when you want to put in a further helping of feed, the mix being just damp enough so that it will cling together long enough to reach the float at the range you are fishing. In other words, this is a cloud bait, but it will be black instead of white. At the start, put one good handful over the float. If fish are present, they will respond almost instantly and will continue to do so provided you keep introducing the feed, the main aim, as you should recall, being to keep samples constantly falling down through the water at all levels. The difference with bloodworm is that it is unlikely the fish will stay in exactly the same place and you will find it necessary to offer the float to one side of the original position, a movement which could reduce your range to as little as 3 m. This doesn't matter so long as you keep the feed landing accurately on top of the float. The French, in this situation, keep switching from one pole to another (all, of course, tackled up in the same way) to change ranges, I have never understood why because moving a 5 m pole about in the manner described should always keep you in touch with some fish because of the way they respond instantly to this kind of feeding. Furthermore, if there's a wind the French persist with a balsa bristle float (Fig. 26) fixed top and bottom and are, thereby, distinctly hampered. With

125

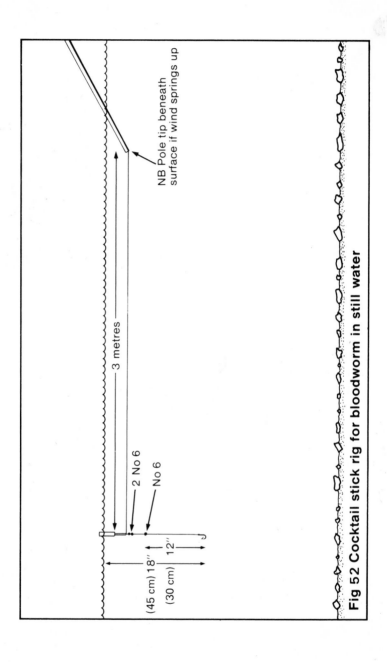

NB Pole tip beneath surface if wind springs up

3 metres

2 No 6

No 6

(45 cm) 18''

(30 cm) 12''

Fig 52 Cocktail stick rig for bloodworm in still water

the cocktail stick (as you can see in Fig. 52), you can bury the line out of the way of the wind and still fish the float in the desired position without interference. The main thing to remember is to keep changing the point at which the hookbait is presented and, if bites are not as instant as I have suggested they should be, increase the amount of feed until fish are contacted. It may also be necessary to change the depth at which you have the tackle set (either up or down) many times during the course of a match, but regardless of how deep it is, you start at the 18 in (45 cm) setting.

The balsa bristle and cocktail stick methods just described add up to the only techniques you need for bloodworm in still waters. Now, the methods for canals and first, the long range method with the balsa bristle float (Fig. 26). The tackle set up is precisely the same as shown for still waters in Fig. 37 the difference being the feeding pattern. Start with four small balls of soil and bloodworm mixed as semi-cloud instead of the ten balls I recommended for still water and then proceed as before.

Our next method in canals calls for the use of the gudgeon float (Fig. 28). It's a close quarters approach which should be fished at a maximum range of 2 m. A commitment to this tackle means that in advance of the match you have decided that a catch of gudgeon, plus, possibly, the odd sizable perch, has a chance of winning. Obviously, the tackle could be fished up to 10 m but, as we would still only be catching gudgeon at that range, there is no point to it. Time would be lost and less fish would result than fishing closer to the bank. Look now at our diagram (Fig. 53) and study the difference between this rig and that recommended for maggot and caster fishing with the same float on canals (Fig. 43). First of all, we are using a crook instead of elastic inside the pole, because we are fishing at close range for small fish. So why fish an elastic for small fish like gudgeon when the main purpose of the elastic with a pole is to give extra protection when a big fish is hooked? That's because those odd perch could

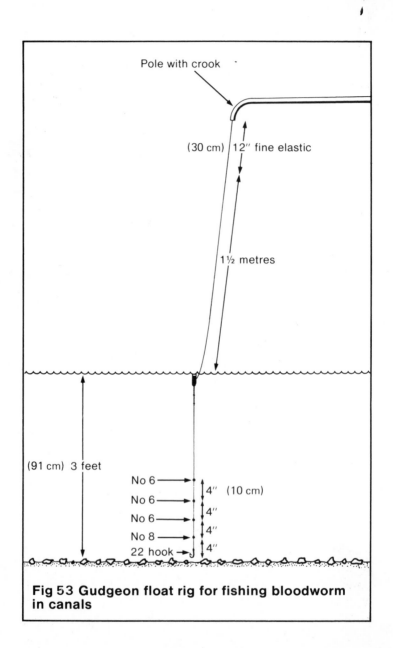

Pole with crook

(30 cm) 12″ fine elastic

1½ metres

(91 cm) 3 feet

No 6
No 6 — 4″ (10 cm)
No 6 — 4″
No 8 — 4″
22 hook — 4″

Fig 53 Gudgeon float rig for fishing bloodworm in canals

also be sizable and we don't want to lose them. Notice, too, the change in the shots, now strung out close to the hook, and the increased distance between float and pole from 24 in (60 cm) to just over 1½ m. In this case, this is not a fixed distance but the right distance for a swim 91 cm deep as shown in the diagram. The idea of this (and if you look carefully at the measurements given you will see exactly what I am driving at) is to ensure that all fish will be brought directly to the hand without unshipping any part of the pole. In other words, the length of line between pole and float is governed solely by the depth being fished and this need to swing fish to the hand. Once the depth is established, you simply subtract that from the length of the pole and the answer is the amount of line you need between pole and float.

Turning to the feeding pattern, the feed medium is clayey soil (what the French call *argile*) riddled fine and dampened just enough to hold firm when gripped. The jokers which should be used with it are added when needed. Don't begin this time with a big helping, just a single walnut-sized ball. Again, bites should be instant. If and as the gudgeon respond, give them another ball the same size every three fish, simply slackening the rate of feed if bites slow.

Our canal methods now complete for bloodworm, let's move finally to the fishing of this bait with the pole on rivers. The choice of float here is the ubiquitous balsa bristle (Fig. 26) or, when additional weight down the line is required, the bodied bristle (Fig. 27), a float we haven't used so far in this book and one selected now for its extra buoyancy. Though the end tackle is similar to that used for still waters (Fig. 37), it's different enough to justify closer examination (Fig. 54), so that the variables at this point are clearly understood. Changes here are all to do with the frequency or otherwise of bites. If the fish are responding satisfactorily, the end tackle should be fished exactly as shown in the diagram. If not, the Olivette and its No 6 stop shot should be moved down to join the tell-

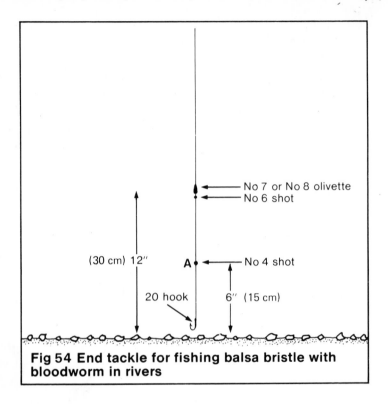

No 7 or No 8 olivette
No 6 shot

(30 cm) 12"   A   No 4 shot

20 hook   6" (15 cm)

Fig 54 End tackle for fishing balsa bristle with bloodworm in rivers

tale, thus concentrating all the weight at point A. That such a concentration of weight so near the hook will have the desired result was something I discovered when the 1977 World Championships were fished in Luxembourg on the River Moselle. This move makes the presentation of the hookbait to a doubting fish more positive. With this method, the bloodworm should be fished on a 20 hook tied to a 1 lb (450 g) hook length which is linked to a 1.5 lb (680 g) main line. In a river, we catch all sorts of fish with the bloodworm though roach, skimmers and bream are the likeliest to respond. And we are not looking for a small catch, either. This rig can easily yield double figures, a statement which, I hope, will further erode the claim that this approach with bloodworm and the pole on a river is wrong, because it cannot produce enough to win a match in England. The possibility of quality fish on a river means that you must fish this method with an elastic instead of a flick tip.

It reminds me of one experience on a river where I fished a peg which had produced 7 lb (3.1 kg) of roach with maggot on a 20 to win a section. As an experiment, I decided after that match to fish the same peg with the bloodworm method we are now discussing and I had 7 lb (3.1 kg) of fish in 90 minutes instead of the five hours the match had lasted. It told me I could win in five hours with bloodworm. My best weight with bloodworm on a river since has been 16 lb (7.25 kg) on the Witham. This won me the match.

The feeding pattern for bloodworm with this rig is exactly the same as the first of the still water methods I gave, that designed to take bigger fish. The difference, of course, is that we are now fishing moving water instead of still, a difference which means that I have found it best to put the *hookbait* in a yard (1m approx.) upstream of the point at which I am introducing the feed so that you are running the bloodworm on the hook *into* the feed pile you have created. No other rig or feeding pattern is necessary with bloodworm on a river, only a switch to the larger bodied bristle float if the strength of the current demands a much larger Olivette to enable you to fish your bait in the manner shown in Fig. 54.

As I am sure you have gathered, I have a great enthusiasm for this bait. As a match angler, I have come to prize it very highly indeed. Equally, I will admit that it is very much a match fishing bait though that, I feel, is because other anglers, particularly the specimen hunters, have not given it sufficient trial, especially as a potential attractor for drawing big fish to their hookbaits.

And talking of bloodworm as the hookbait, there are different ways in which it can be presented on the hook, not just on its own, but also using Mystic, the well-known French bait paste, in its red colour. For newcomers, I thought it would be useful (Fig. 55) to show some of these

131

Fig. 55 Hooking bloodworm and the use of Mystic: a) the main approach when fishing bloodworm is to hook the bait in the head.

different presentations, for small changes on the hook can prove positive when using the pole methods I've just described. The pictures are, I feel, self-explanatory but it would be wrong if I did not add that while the French

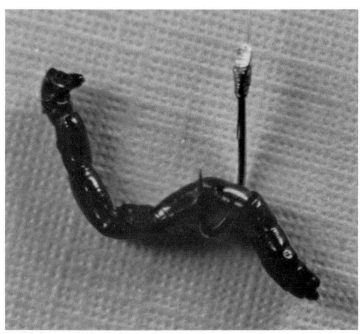

b) When fish are biting shyly (or nipping the bait's tail), the bloodworm can be middle hooked, another variation of this being to partially thread the blood-worm onto the hook. Two, three, or even four bloodworms can be offered in this way.

132

c) Mystic is an artificial paste much favoured by French anglers in its red form as an imitation bloodworm. Available at most good English tackle shops, Mystic fulfils two purposes: if fish are coming quickly it saves hooking time (upwards of 20 fish can be caught on one hook loading) and it is often better when big fish are being encountered, either on its own or as a cocktail with other baits. There is a right and a wrong way to fish Mystic when offered on its own.

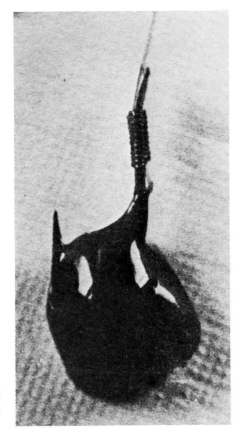

d) The wrong way is to wrap it round the bend and shank so that the barb remains visible.

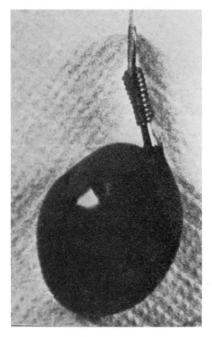

e) The right way is to wrap it on so that a neat ball covers barb, bend and most of the shank.

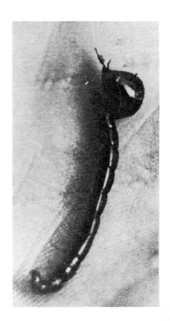

f) A cocktail of Mystic and bloodworm is reckoned very effective by continental anglers for sizeable roach in rivers.

g) A cocktail of Mystic and maggot is rated good for bream.

have great confidence in red Mystic as an alternative to the bloodworm itself, I have not so far enjoyed results which allow me to share that enthusiasm. That doesn't mean you shouldn't try it for yourself!

Finally, I feel sadly obliged to conclude this chapter with a warning that bloodworm is a banned bait on all too many waters in this country and, worse still, more bans seem to be being introduced as time goes by. For this reason, you should obviously check carefully before using it on any given water to make sure it is permitted. Various reasons are advanced for these bans, ranging from amazing claims that bloodworm (the most natural bait there is) harms the fish, to the oldest of all, that anglers not prepared to go to the trouble of collecting bloodworms should not be beaten by those who are. I have no time for these arguments or, indeed, for bait bans of any kind, for they are invariably applied for the wrong reasons.

9 Pole Methods for Special Situations

Under this heading, I want to discuss some pole methods which are not generally applicable like those discussed earlier in this book. They are, however, necessary should you find yourself fishing the pole in the situations I am about to describe.

The first concerns a fish most anglers consider a nuisance, the bleak. For the match angler, however, bleak can be a winning species and, therefore, he must always take them into account, especially when these are the only fish to be caught in his peg. Though there are bleak in still waters, they are likely to assume more importance in rivers, especially when there is some fresh water running through for this seems to galvanise bleak into feeding madly. In still waters, they can be encountered at any time. In both situations, the main point is that you should only fish for them if you are convinced they will produce the best possible weight from the swim drawn on the day. If you think any other species is capable of this, then, clearly, you should forget altogether about the bleak.

As bleak are mostly feeders at the surface, that part of any water where fish are always hardest to catch, special tackles have to be used for them, and those for the pole angler are no exception.

The tackle (Fig. 56) is fished with a flick tip pole. The float is a short piece of solid plastic 2 in (5 cm) long. Some anglers use similar lengths of peacock quill for this purpose, but I find plastic better for it adds extra weight to a tackle

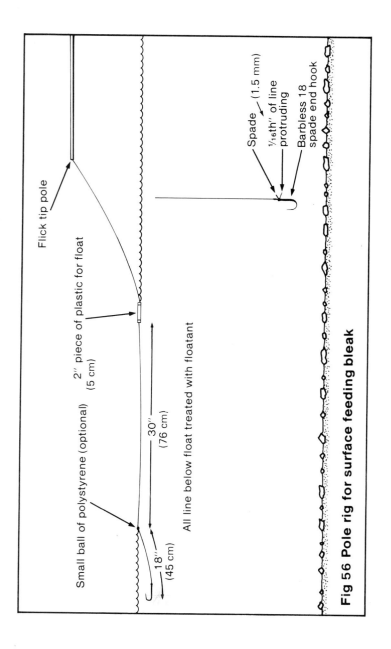

Fig 56 Pole rig for surface feeding bleak

Flick tip pole

2" piece of plastic for float
(5 cm)

Small ball of polystyrene (optional)

30"
(76 cm)

18"
(45 cm)

All line below float treated with floatant

Spade (1.5 mm)

1/16th" of line protruding

Barbless 18 spade end hook

137

mostly fished with no weight down the line, thus making it easier to cast to the desired location. The whole of the line between float and hook is greased with line floatant. Again, some anglers prefer to crinkle the line between their finger nails just below the float to enable them to see it more easily, but I find this unnecessary and prefer the floating line.

The best bait for bleak bashing is maggot and it should be offered on a barbless 18 spade end hook tied to a 1.5 lb (680 g) hook length with a 2 lb (907 g) line. To prevent maggots being blown up the line, leave ¹⁄₁₆ in (1.5 mm) of line standing proud from the hook (see Fig. 56 again), when the hook has been whipped onto the line. Maggots blown up the line slow your catch rate. As you can see, the lower 4 ft (1.2 m) of line is greased. This is shown for clarity's sake with just the lower end carrying the hook below the surface.

To catch surface-feeding bleak, a constant stream of loose fed maggots is necessary with the float cast to the same point as the maggots. Not only are bleak attracted by the maggots, they are, in my opinion, attracted by anything on the surface when they are in feeding mood, including the float. So there's no need to worry about any splash it may cause. The splash is an attraction. It doesn't matter, either, if the line falls in a heap behind the float when you cast in. Bleak bite savagely and they'll easily straighten out that line. And it is this straightening of the line you watch for and *not* the movement of the float as the signal to strike. The float is merely being used as the vehicle to get your bait where you want it to be. If you do see the float move, it's most likely that your strike will turn out to be too late and the fish will have dropped the bait.

If bites are maintained at a good rate, stay with the constant loose feed. If they slow, start using fine cloud groundbait.

Finally on this tackle, what about that optional ball of polythene I've shown in our diagram? When it's windy and the line becomes difficult to see, this becomes your float to indicate bites. It's small enough to see and not big enough to impede the tackle in any way. It's held in place by the knot which links the hook length to the main line.

Our second bleak tackle (Fig. 57) is the one to use when bleak are taking just under as opposed to on the surface. The float to use is the smallest size of gudgeon float (Fig. 28). In our diagram (Fig. 57), I have shown the rig fished for a start at a depth of 12 in (30 cm) with a single micro shot pinched on exactly half way between float and hook,

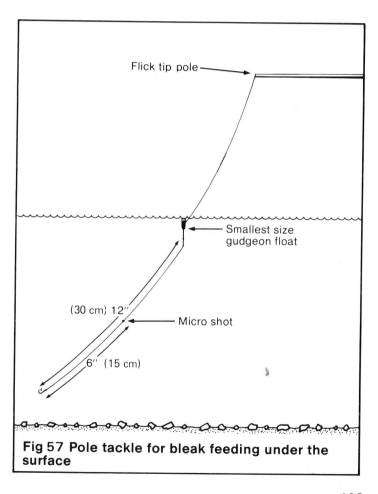

Flick tip pole

Smallest size
gudgeon float

(30 cm) 12″

Micro shot

6″ (15 cm)

Fig 57 Pole tackle for bleak feeding under the surface

the latter again an 18 barbless spade end with the small piece of line left projecting as in Fig. 56. Now, instead of watching the line for bites as we did when surface feeding, we are now looking for the usual submersion of the float. The loose feeding process is the same as before, the only other thing to mention being that the length of line below the float may be increased up to a maximum of 3 ft (91 cm). Bleak can lie at varying levels in the surface layers and it's to catch fish moving up and down in those levels that this tackle has been designed, the trick, of course, being to keep extending and contracting this piece of line to stay in touch with them as much as you possibly can. If bites don't result or slacken, go deeper until you reach 3 ft (91 cm) then start shortening off again. It is amazing how often you find yourself having to make adjustments in this way during a session of bleak fishing.

The next special occasion float is what I call the Ulster though it is, in fact, a large bodied balsa bristle (Fig. 27). The name stems from the fact that this float has come to the fore in Northern Ireland where anglers fishing the spring match festivals on the River Erne in and around Enniskillen and the River Bann at Portadown have regularly recorded weights of more than 100 lb and, latterly, more than 200 lb. Most of these were on the pole, the weapon once condemned by so many as a small-fish, small-catch tool. When I won the famous Benson and Hedges three-day Festival on the Erne in 1978 with 332 lb (150.5 kg) from three matches, I took every single fish with the pole simply because no English method can compete when fish, big and small, are to be caught as quickly as they can be on these marvellous waters. Since then I have won the final of the Fermanagh Festival with 205 lb (93 kg) in the same way. Before the pole took over in Ulster matches, anglers used the waggler or the leger with rod and reel, but they soon found out there was no way they could compete with the pole for speed, with anglers using the method I am now going to describe.

Compared with the delicate tackles, we have discussed

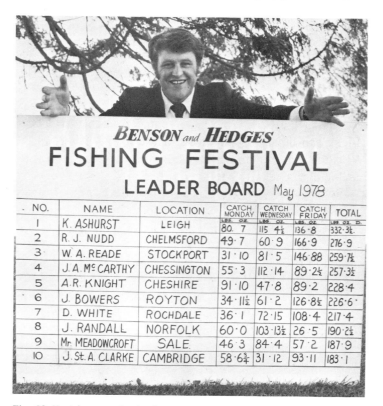

BENSON and HEDGES
FISHING FESTIVAL
LEADER BOARD May 1978

NO.	NAME	LOCATION	CATCH MONDAY	CATCH WEDNESDAY	CATCH FRIDAY	TOTAL
			LBS. OZ.	LBS. OZ.	LBS. OZ.	LBS. OZ. D.
1	K. ASHURST	LEIGH	80. 7	115 4½	136·8	332·3½.
2	R. J. NUDD	CHELMSFORD	49·7	60·9	166·9	276·9
3	W. A. READE	STOCKPORT	31·10	81·5	146·88	259·7½
4	J. A. McCARTHY	CHESSINGTON	55·3	112·14	89·2½	257·3½
5	A. R. KNIGHT	CHESHIRE	91·10	47·8	89·2	228·4
6	J. BOWERS	ROYTON	34·11½	61·2	126·8½	226·6·
7	D. WHITE	ROCHDALE	36·1	72·15	108·4	217·4
8	J. RANDALL	NORFOLK	60·0	103·13½	26·5	190·2½
9	Mr. MEADOWCROFT	SALE	46·3	84·4	57·2	187·9
10	J. St. A. CLARKE	CAMBRIDGE	58·6¾	31·12	93·11	183·1

Fig. 58 Kevin's name heads the prize list at the 1978 Benson and Hedges Festival in Ulster — the event that led to the perfection of the rig shown in Fig. 59.

for other situations with the pole, this is crude gear indeed but, on the waters I have just mentioned, it is totally effective, though mostly appealing to match anglers intent on winning big money prizes. The diagram (Fig. 59) tells you most of what you need to know in terms of specifications. The float of course is a giant of its type and usually about 6 in (15 cm) in length in the body. I have only two comments to make. The first concerns the difference in the main weight, a barrel lead instead of an Olivette. These are used simply because they are easier to trim to make them balance exactly with the float, Olivettes, you will remember, being too hard to adapt in this way. The lead is held in

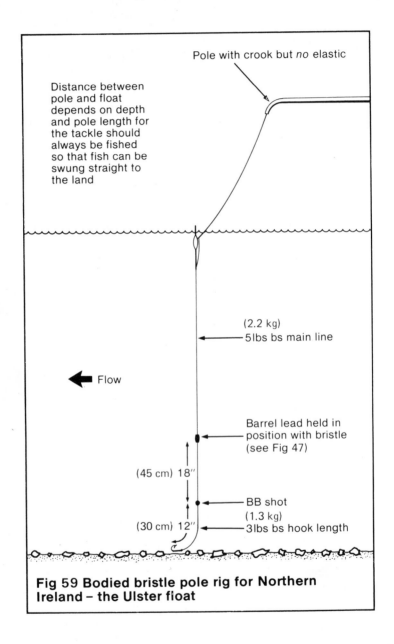

Pole with crook but *no* elastic

Distance between pole and float depends on depth and pole length for the tackle should always be fished so that fish can be swung straight to the land

(2.2 kg)
5lbs bs main line

Flow

Barrel lead held in position with bristle (see Fig 47)

(45 cm) 18″

BB shot
(1.3 kg)
3lbs bs hook length

(30 cm) 12″

Fig 59 Bodied bristle pole rig for Northern Ireland – the Ulster float

place with a piece of bristle, not a shot. But while this is a question of convenience, it's worth adding that the barrel leads do make it easier to cast. The other point to note is that while we are using a pole with a crook, we are not using elastic, even though we expect to encounter better fish. The top of the main line is fixed directly to the crook and the reason we are able to fish in this way is the strength of the main line (5 lb (2.2 kg) bs) and the hook length (3 lb (1.3 kg) bs), calibres which make it possible to swing fish up to 1 lb (450 g) in weight straight to the hand. That could not be done if any elastic had been incorporated into the tackle. This is also why we fix the line with a crook. It gives us extra rigidity in a situation where it's most definitely needed. The tackle is effective in depths as shallow as 3 ft (91 cm) on up to 12 ft (3.6 m) with the hookbait, without exception, being maggot, usually fished in multiples of two or three on a 12 hook. For feeding, the bread groundbait should be of a heavy consistency laced with maggots and casters, this heavy mix being all right in even the shallowest swims — the casters, as always when maggot is the hookbait, being the attractors for bigger fish. Start with two or three balls of groundbait and keep topping this up at intervals as fish are caught. If there is any lack of response (and that can happen even in Ulster!), it's almost certainly the groundbait that is doing the damage. The message is to switch to loose feed in large quantities. One would think nothing, for instance, of feeding an entire gallon of loose feed in a match here, or even two gallons if they're really on!

The pole range at which to plan an attack with these Ulster fish is 5 m. As the match progresses, you would hope, as a result of careful placement of the feed, to bring fish closer than this and so speed up your catch rate still further. There are occasions, however, when, instead of moving in, they move out and obviously you must then increase the length of pole being fished to stay in touch. If the wind here is very strong (upstream or downstream, the former being the most difficult), the Ulster float should be fixed bottom only and fished loose like a waggler. This enables the line to be buried under the surface. The end tackle remains the same as in Fig. 59.

On the other hand, it must be admitted that this tackle works best on the Ulster rivers when they are stationary or flowing only sluggishly. Whenever any real flow develops, these pole rigs begin to lose their effectiveness. The fish seem to decide that they don't want a bait fished at the speed of the flow but will only take it when stationary. That's the signal for a change to the bung float (Fig. 31) and you simply go through the same progressions of fishing with this German float as I gave for English rivers as shown in Fig. 47 and described in Chapter 6. But do remember to work to the line strengths shown here — 5 lb (2.2 kg) main line, 3 lb (1.3 kg) hook length — and not those cited in our earlier discussion of this float.

In conclusion, there's one other thing that needs saying about the Ulster float and that is that I know nowhere in England where it could be considered relevant to angling needs. As its name suggests its current virtue is only applicable to the Ulster waters.

10 Summary

As I have said more than once in this book, old habits die
hard with anglers, the delay in taking up the pole being
just the most recent example of this kind of conservatism.
In my own case, you must have noticed that, during the
early 1970s, I conducted a sort of on-off flirtation with
the method until finally accepting it for the great addition
to the angling arsenal that it is. Though this happened
some time ago, I received what I consider the most signifi-
cant seal of approval two years ago, and I'd like to tell you
about it now in the hope that it will convince any remaining
doubters. As readers will know, my surname was well-
known in angling circles long before I began fishing, thanks
to the exploits of my father, Benny Ashurst. He was and
still is a great match angler and, as you can imagine, he has
always been an inspiration to me. My father, however, was
one of the doubters and, during my early years of experi-
mentation with the pole, he would scoff, dismissing it as
being 20 years behind the times. On that day two years
ago, my father was 66 (he's happily still going strong), and
we were fishing a match on the Liverpool end of the Leeds
and Liverpool Canal. I had won my section – fishing the
pole. My father had been beaten by the anglers on both
sides of him, both of them also using poles. He had come
up to my peg at the end of the match and, after listening
to the usual tale of how I had got on, stood thoughtfully
for a few minutes before turning to me and saying with no
little emphasis, 'You know what, Kevin, I shall have to get
me a pole'. From him, that was an accolade and I knew

more certainly than ever that I had been right to spend so many hours in perfecting my own technique with the method.

Next, I would like to repeat another statement made earlier for it deserves re-emphasis as it is so important. That is to ignore those who would have you believe that you must slavishly copy the continentals if you are to be successful with the pole. That's because, as I hope I have demonstrated, there is now most definitely an English dimension in pole fishing and it is far better to follow this lead for success on the waters you fish regularly, because most of our fishing is not the same as theirs. It is for this reason that I had what some may feel an important change of heart when finally getting down to committing these words to paper. I had planned to include in this book a selection of continental tackles as used by some of the great French anglers, these being kindly offered by my old friend, Daniel Maury, editor of 'La Pêche et Les Poissons', France's best known angling magazine. Though Daniel may disagree with me, I decided against this course for the more I looked at the details of these tackles the more convinced I became that their inclusion here would have been merely academic. In other words, while they did have relevance in France, they had none here, or none that couldn't be dealt with by using the methods I have included in this book. Some of them are fished in exactly the same manner on the continent, a statement which should tell you that I have been selective, using the tackles I felt had an application here and rejecting those that didn't. The main thing is not to be tempted by the more complex continental rigs into believing that their very complexity will bring you success. That is why I must repeat that I cannot imagine any of the circumstances I have outlined in this book in which the tackles given will not provide the answer you need though, obviously, no tackle will do this if our friends, the fish, choose to go on a hunger strike.

These remarks also have bearing on another statement I made, that the pole simplifies fishing. It really does do just

146

that, so why introduce complexities unnecessarily? I am sure I need say no more on that point.

Now another earlier statement of equal importance, the need to understand that the pole fishing method is *not* a substitute for the time-honoured English approach with rod and reel, but a compliment to it. The angler who can fish both methods well must be a better angler for he is more equipped to cope with the changing conditions and the changing moods and habits of the fish themselves.

Furthermore, the pole *cannot* be a substitute for rod and reel simply because, as we have seen, it does have a limited range. At anything beyond 12 m, it cannot, at the moment compete. Within its range, however, it can not only be a substitute for rod and reel, it can be *better*. That's because the delicate presentation it permits of a bait will tempt finicky fish when the rod and reel approach fails. Indeed, it's no bad idea to adopt the policy that if fish are difficult and within reach, then the pole is a must from the outset. Also the pole can no longer be dismissed as a method only fit for days when small catches are the likely result. Nor can it still be said that it was only good for fishing bloodworms for small fish. As the Ulster rivers have demonstrated, truly enormous bags of fish can be put together with the pole while, here in England, the blood-worm and pole myth has been completely demolished. Again, I'm sure I need say no more.

As everybody knows, I am principally a match angler and it is in this setting that I have made the greatest use of the pole. It could be argued with some reason that the pole is really only for match fishing. Accepting this argument for the moment, I think too many match anglers still aren't using poles and I'm not just talking about those who fish the richer open events. That statement goes for all match anglers, right down to those who restrict their activities to the smallest club events. Indeed, I'd say the latter are among those who could score most with the pole. On the other hand, I don't support the idea that pole fishing is only for match anglers, simply because I cannot believe that any angler can fail to use and experience the finesse of the pole without enjoying it for its own sake. It's a pleasure not to be missed which is why I commend it so strongly to all.

Next, I'd like to mention something not so far discussed, the use by some anglers of flick tip poles for the quivertip method of legering, particularly on rivers. I cannot see the point of it because it is simply not necessary. If you are quivertipping at a certain range with the pole, you can also float leger at the same range (as in Fig. 45 and 48) and that is much the better method. It produces better bite indication than the quivertip and, therefore, must be given priority.

For those who are newcomers to the pole, I'd like to conclude by re-emphasising a number of points of importance when it comes to using the pole for the first time. In no particular order, I'd mention first the need to plumb the depth at the start. Yes, I know it's something almost every angler does without thinking but, in this setting where exactness is very much the name of the game, accurate plumbing is essential. You have only to look back at some of the tackles I've recommended to see that if this isn't done, the tackle will not fulfil the purpose for which it was designed. Every time you take a tackle off a winder, plumb the depth before you do anything else. As the advertising jingle says — you know it makes sense. Next, always make up your pole tackles so that the hook is on a length of line of a lesser breaking strain than the main line linking it to the pole tip. While anglers have always done this because, rightly, they believe that fish can see a trap if thick, heavy lines are dangled in front of their noses, this lighter line ensures that if you have a break it's usually at the point where hook length and main line are joined. While the same thing would happen when fishing with a rod and reel, in the pole setting it means that a complete tackle hasn't been ruined or lost. All you have to do to repair it is simply re-tie a new hook length.

Remember, too, what I said about starting your pole fishing at no more than 5 m. It's good advice for it's easier to handle a short pole than a long one and handling is something at which you should feel really adept before trying to fish beyond this range. At the same time, try and develop a new perspective about length, the length of your pole and the length of the tackle and how the two are interrelated. This will tell you if unshipping is necessary and exactly where to break the pole to achieve this movement with the greatest efficiency. It will, of course, also tell you whether it is feasible to swing the fish directly to your hand, always the best course if depth and range permit.

In urging you to stick to the float patterns I have given, I'd like first to remind you of the number of mentions the balsa bristle float (Fig. 26) has been given compared to the rest. That's because this float, designed by Robert Tesse and therefore very definitely one instance where it's paid to follow the continental approach, is so versatile. Some of the other floats will not be used nearly so often and others, as we have seen, are very definitely occasional floats. It's up to you to decide which have a relevance for the waters you fish regularly and to put together a collection of tackles on winders which will cover you for all pole fishing eventualities at those waters. Each size of float should be made up so that it is available in all the line strengths needed, with and without elastics where relevant, and with the different sizes of hook required. Still on floats, a word is necessary, I think, about the amount of float which should show above the surface when pole fishing — as anglers say, how much is 'dotted'. Far too often, one sees anglers with much more of the float sticking proudly out of the water than is necessary. Such a float is more difficult for a biting fish to submerge than a float which is correctly dotted. For some of the pole float patterns, it is necessary for total sensitivity to have just a little of the bristle on the top of the float showing. In Fig. 60 I have shown exactly how all the floats in this book should be dotted so as to fish at their best. Weight your floats to fish in this way and you'll be doing things right from the start. Though it shouldn't need saying, always use the tackle designed for

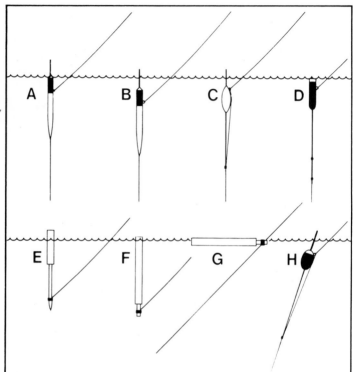

A When fished with all baits other than bloodworm, the balsa bristle should be dotted so that the white collar and the bristle show at the surface

B When the balsa bristle is fished with bloodworm, only a section of the bristle should show

C The bodied bristle

D The gudgeon float

E The cocktail stick

F The dibber is dotted like this when the conditions, especially the wind, are adverse

G The dibber lies flat on the surface when conditions are ideal

H As it is held back when being fished, the bung float is always dotted at an angle like this with just the tip (and not the body) showing

Fig 60 Dotting pole floats correctly

the job in hand. Don't try and make any of these tackles work in a setting in which they were not meant to be used. They simply won't work. It's for this reason that I tried to deal with them in a logical order so that you could work out your own equation for picking the right tackle.

My last reminder is not to do with tackle . . . but with feed. Never overdo it for it's as fatal with a pole as it is with any other method. Though wise anglers may consider that an unnecessary statement, it remains one of the commonest errors made by anglers and particularly those who are just beginning in the game. Think of feeding in the same way as you would about serving a meal. You don't serve the main course until your guests have eaten the soup. In just the same way, there is no point offering fish anything more to eat until you are reasonably certain they have eaten what they have already been given and if, like Mr Bumble, you've been as stingy as he was with Oliver Twist that could be so much the better.

In conclusion, I can only hope that anyone who takes up pole fishing as a result of reading this book will gain as much pleasure — and profit! — from it as I have done.

Postscript

Even before the foregoing chapters were completed, I had already begun practising for the 1982 World Championships which were to be fished in the September of that year on the Newry Canal in Northern Ireland. As most readers will be aware, I went on to fulfil a lifetime's ambition in the Championships themselves . . . by becoming World Champion. What those who so kindly congratulated me at the time did not realise was that while I was as delighted as they seemed to be at my win, inside I was doubly delighted at what, for me, had been the greatest possible reward I could have desired for the years of practise and study I had put into pole fishing. Without that I would not be World Champion and this, I like to hope, will give still more weight to the things I have been saying earlier in this book.

I think it is important to tell the story of what happened, partly because this seems as good a place as any to record it, but mostly because it could inspire others to carry on the good work, not just in the World Championships for England but at all levels of match fishing in this country.

From the first moment I heard that the match was to be on the Newry Canal, the water which links Newry with Lough Neagh to the north and Carlingford Lough and the sea to the south, I was convinced it would be a pole fishing match.

Indeed, in a magazine article at that time I criticised the organisers for picking it on the grounds that, by this selection, they had made a gift of the event to the continental pole teams . . . even though I had never fished it!

Fig. 61 Well wishers carry Kevin from the banks of the Newry Canal after his Championship win.

Soon after this, I was at my hotel when fishing one of the excellent festivals they have in Ulster when I got into a heated discussion with the Irish team manager, Oliver McGauley, on this point. He was very upset and demanded to know how I could present such a verdict on a water I hadn't even seen, never mind not having fished it. I replied that I didn't need to see it and felt perfectly happy about basing my statement on my knowledge of past results there and my knowledge of just what the continentals were capable of and, more important, just how much use they would make of those capabilities when it came to the match itself. I recall my exact words. 'It's just made for them,' I told Oliver. I regret to add that we finished up not the best of friends, possibly because I accused Olly of influencing the choice because Newry just happens to be his home town.

Despite my reservations about the water, which was first opened in 1741 and is one of Britain's oldest canals, I nursed my annual hope that I would be picked for England to fish the match and, for this reason, decided to make the canal's aquaintance at the earliest possible moment.

This came shortly after the 1981 World Championships on the Warwickshire Avon in England. We had finished a disappointing second to the old enemy, France, on a water on which we had been rated certainties, a rating which was not fulfilled because of the appalling weather conditions which prevented the river fishing to its normal form. It was a bad memory and I was happy to turn my attention to the next challenge – the 1982 event.

I was going to Ireland in the following month, October, to fish the Cootehill Championships and decided to travel early to give me the opportunity of fishing the Newry Canal. Once there, a friendly Irishman offered to show me the water and, while he couldn't tell me exactly where the World Championships were going to be fished, he took me to a spot where the regulars normally caught fish.

I set up a ten metre pole. The float was a balsa bristle (Fig. 26), now widely known as a carrot. The hook was a 20 linked to the pole by a 1 lb (.4 kg) bs hook length and a 1½ lb (.6 kg) main line and set for the short line method, ie the distance from pole tip to float was just 18 in (45 cm). The Olivette was a No 6 and the bait was double blood-worm. I began by putting in ten balls of feed, groundbait and soil mixed together and laced with bloodworms. There had been an overnight frost and there was no wind. After 15 minutes I caught a small bream but the next 15 minutes were not productive. I decided to move the tell-tale shot so that it was just 3 in (75 cm) off the deck. That was the answer. The fish started responding and, after about four hours, I reckon I had 25 lb (11 kg) in the net. Not bad, thought I. For the week before, the Irish had fished two team trials for the World match and just 3 lb (1.3 kg) had won them both.

At the same time, I dismissed maggot as a bait. It was going to be a bloodworm job and events again proved me right.

In spring 1982, the England team manager, Stan Smith, staged a series of trials on the Canal and, again, everything pointed to the pole and bloodworm. Soon after those trials, he picked his team and I was fortunate enough to be selected again. The team was something of a sensation for, apart from Ivan Marks of Leicester, all the other members of the squad were from the north west, the only part of the country where, you will remember, there had been any tradition of bloodworm use. Apart from myself, the other north western men were Dave Brogden (Preston), former World Champion Ian Heaps (Stockport), Alan McAtee (Bolton) and Dave Roper (Preston). In naming those names, Stan had made it clear that he was picking pole and bloodworm anglers because the water demanded this and making 1982 the first time an England team had gone into a World Championship pledged solely to the method the continentals had used for so long.

Two weeks before the match, this squad went to the Canal again to practise. Naturally, we tried the maggot and found we could catch with it on the pole but not with normal English running line tackle. We also found yet again that bloodworm caught more fish. An individual fishing on his own could get 25 lb (11 kg) in three hours, but when fishing in a group (the situation which would prevail in the match), catches were not so good with the end pegs the best. Dave Roper had the best weight during this practise of 18 lb (8.1 kg) from an end peg. The best weight from a middle peg was 17 lb (7.7 kg).

Such basic matters settled, we went on to make other discoveries. If we fished the balsa bristle with a No 6

Fig. 62 Tackling up for the World Championships

Olivette, as I had done the previous October, we caught smaller bream and roach. If we used a 10 with the bodied bristle (Fig. 27), a scaled down version of the Ulster tackle described in Chapter 9, we found that not only did we catch faster but we got bigger fish.

All this led us to our policy for the match. Each man was to set up two 10 metre carbon poles with a balsa bristle, a short line setting, an 8 Olivette 12 in (30 cm) from an 18 hook and a No 4 tell-tale mid-way between hook and Olivette. A third 10 metre carbon pole was to be set up with the bodied bristle tackle, again with a short line. The business end was a 10 Olivette 12 in (30 cm) from the hook with a BB equidistant between them. Each man was to throw 12 orange size balls of bait laced with bloodworm during the five-minute pre-baiting period and no more – regardless of what the continentals put in.

In the team match on the Saturday, I was well pleased. I drew a peg where I had caught 17 lb (7.7 kg) which we had already christened the Bo-peep swim. That was because I'd left a box of matches of that make there after catching those fish and they were still there when next we visited it. So pleased was I with this peg that I told Stan Smith that this was one section he could count on winning. Section wins, of course, being the most important factor in the team match for it's the team with the best score over the sections which take the title.

When the signal for pre-baiting sounded, I put in the 12 balls we had agreed. I held my pole in the left hand and threw the feed with my right to make sure it went exactly to the right place – where the float was going to fish. I had finished three minutes before the rest. As always, the continentals were putting it in like there was no tomorrow, 20, 30 and even 40 balls, this being the main reason why the canal did not fish as well as it might.

I started off on the pole with the Ulster style tackle, so confident was I my draw would bring me big fish. It was, I told myself, going to be a mere formality. On my second cast, I had a 3 oz (85 g) roach. Ten minutes later, I got

Fig. 63 Kevin swings in one of the smallest roach with which he opened his account in the World individual championship.

another small fish. After that, it was a struggle. Going into the second hour of the three hour match, I had six fish for about 1 lb (450 g) in the net. So much for vain hopes! In that second hour, however, I started to pick up roach and skimmers fairly steadily. The opposition on either side, Austria on my left and San Marino on my right, were still struggling. With 90 minutes to go, I entered my best spell. I was still getting the same stamp of fish, but more often. My early confidence dissipated, I had persuaded myself that it was going to be a waiting game. These fish were the reward, I felt, for my patience. At the scales, I had 6 lb 6½ oz (2.89 kg). I had kept my promise to Stan by winning the section and, better still, I shared with a Czech competitor the honour of having taken the biggest weight in the team match.

Immediately, friends began saying it was a pity I had done this on the wrong day. In the past, of course, when there was only one match, the angler with the biggest weight in the team match was the individual champion. To become champion nowadays, there is still another match to be won the following day. That night I told myself that if I drew well I would win that one, too.

As always, the next day's individual match was to be fished on a different section of the water. We all knew where the pegs had been placed and I wanted to be drawn between 30 and 40 which was towards the upstream end of the length in question. There was a tree in that ten peg length which I knew marked a good spot and I asked Stan Smith to make sure he drew that one for me. He pulled 37 – dead in front of that tree! I'm sure I needn't say more.

So badly had heavy feeding affected the water the previous day that I decided to cut back on the pre-baiting period this time. It was going to be hard with in all likelihood, a low weight winner. I put in just seven or eight small balls, telling myself that if the fish did go mad I could always top this feed up.

I began with the same tackle I had used the previous day, the modified Ulster rig with the bodied bristle. I got no response at all. It was as if the canal was devoid of fish. Next, I decided to fish an English sliding float rig at a range of 25 yards (22.9 m) with rod and reel. I was now desperate for anything. Still no response. After 15 minutes, I reverted to the pole. By now an hour had gone. I had nothing and I heard that the San Marino angler at the end peg was catching.

Perhaps the lighter tackle on the balsa bristle pole was the answer? Maybe that would find me a small fish or two? After precisely one hour and twenty-five minutes, I had my first bite on this rig. It was a roach weighing exactly half an ounce (14 g). That, I thought, was a great start! Ninety minutes to go and that was the size of fish I might expect. What a good job it wasn't a size limit match! Another fifteen minutes passed before I got another roach of the same size. We were now going into the final hour and I had 1 oz (28 g) in my net. Obviously, this was developing into another waiting game!

Twenty minutes later, I had two more roach. The total weight was now 4 oz (113 g). When I caught them, however, I became convinced there were bigger fish present. It's a hunch only a matchman can understand but I felt it very strongly. For this reason, I put down the pole with the balsa bristle rig and reverted to the Ulster style tackle. I thought that if there really were better fish to be had then my No 10 Olivette would get me down through the small ones to them. I should add that the bankside 'telegraph' had reported similar struggles elsewhere. This meant that mine was not the only treasured draw to take a nosedive and, despite the fact that there was now so little time left, it really was still anybody's match, and with a low weight, too.

I began to become World Champion twenty minutes from the end. That minute marked the start of a sequence of eleven fish, ten roach and one skimmer of about 3 oz (85 g). My biggest fish was a 6 oz (170 g) roach. Just as it had the previous day, my patience had paid off for at the scales my collection of small stuff weighed 1 lb 12¾ oz (820g) – enough on this poorest of poor days to win the match. I made it by a margin of just 5 oz (140 g) over Micky Thill, the England-based angler who fished this match for the USA. It was, of course, the most important 5 oz I had ever caught and proved, far from the first time, just how careful you have got to be in a difficult match, a point I emphasised in earlier chapters. I am equally certain that if I had fished running line tackle in this match, I would have come nowhere, proving the other point I have repeatedly made, that when it's hard the pole is invariably going to be the best approach and bloodworm the likeliest hookbait. I was so pleased about it all, I ended up singing 'Irish Eyes are Smiling' to the assembled crowd accom-

Fig. 64 Kevin with the 1 lb 12¾ ozs catch which made him World Champion on the Newry Canal.

panied by an Irish jazz band. I know I fished better than I sang.

If readers asked me the main lesson from this experience of mine I've got to say it's that I started off as pole angling novice and ended up World Champion. That is the kind of success that can be yours if you develop your skills with the methods I have described. It also emphasised once more the versatility of the balsa bristle family of floats.

Fig. 65 Kevin with the 6 lbs 6½ ozs which made him equal top weight in the World team championships.

Clearly, they are going to remain key floats in any pole angler's arsenal.

I'm happy to add that I am the first English angler to become World Champion using the pole. My four predecessors, the late Billy Lane in 1963, Robin Harris in 1969, Ian Heaps in 1975 and Dave Thomas in 1981, all did it with rod and reel. I take equal pleasure from the fact that

Fig. 66 A thoughtful Kevin packs his gear away after winning the World individual championship.

163

I was also the first angler to win an English open match with the pole.

I say this not to make you say 'he's the greatest' but because I hope these achievements will persuade many more to try and follow my example.

As I said earlier, this was the first World Championship in which an England team had committed themselves totally to the pole. It won't be the last. It's proved too often to be the winning method. So far, team success with it has gone to continental sides. This is why I say we should in future only fish with rod and reel if we are sure it's going to bring us big fish at range. Any indication, however slight, that that is not going to happen should lead to an instant switch to the pole for, whatever happens, you are still going to be on even terms with the others. My view, shared by Stan Smith, is that we are going to fish more World Championships like this one on the Newry Canal. That means the demand for good pole anglers will increase for, as the history of the World Championships demonstrates, many more of the venues have been difficult waters than they have been easy ones.

My only regret about the Championship that brought me the title was, of course, that a team win again evaded England. As everybody knows, Holland won, France were second and we were third and we are still waiting for our first win. Speaking personally, I would far rather that match in Ulster had produced a win for the team than just for me. But there's another time and, with more lessons learnt, we are sure to get there eventually.

In the meantime, if you've read this book and you really want to become proficient with the pole, put plenty of time and effort into it and who knows? You could end up like me . . . at this moment in time the happiest angler in the world.

Index